Living the Dream

CONFESSIONS OF A TRAINEE DETECTIVE

JADE CAMERON

First published in 2025

Cover design: Robert Jarocki
Page Design and Typesetting: Paul Baillie-Lane

This book is memoir. It reflects the author's present recollections of experiences over time. Some names and characteristics have been changed, some events have been compressed, and some dialogue has been recreated.

Paperback ISBN: 978-1-0684383-0-1
eBook ISBN: 978-1-0684383-1-8

CONTENTS

INTRODUCTION

During my time as a detective at Thames Valley Police, I noticed an odd ritual. Whenever you went up to someone and asked, 'how are you?' they would reply with 'living the dream'. It was an ironic running joke that people copied from each other. This book is about my experience of living the dream.

In this book I want to give you an insight into the realities of being a trainee police officer and police detective. In part, it's a response to those borderline glamourous "real policing" shows you see on TV or those heroic recruitment ads. They don't tell you half the story.

I want to give you an honest account of my time in the police to help demystify the role and give those with an interest in policing a more realistic picture of what things are like. Because so many of the best-selling memoirs and the famous stories are all about big, dramatic moments, it's easy to think that police work must be full of them. And though I had my share of action, most of my time was spent on things that the other stories gloss over. Some of it is thankless and more of it than should be is frustrating.

It's also a little bit about catharsis. My time in the police contained some of the most stressful and demoralising times of my life, which took a toll on my physical and mental health; and telling my story like this is a part of getting it all out of my system. Yet, being a police officer was still a defining time of my life. It was a dream I pursued for years, a dream that I ultimately achieved, and then abandoned. My story covers the good, the bad, and everything in between.

It's definitely not my intention to cast judgement on the police who keep us safe. My experiences in the police were shaped by a system that's under pressure from every angle, and which puts unbelievable pressure on the people in it. Just as I did before my time in the police, I have enormous respect for police officers, and am grateful for the work they do.

There are a few areas where I explain the details of some elements of the law and the criminal justice system. I do want to make it plain that I am not a lawyer, and I didn't want to turn this into a legal textbook, so I've simplified my explanations in ways that may sometimes leave out some of the nuances of certain laws. You can always search online for the exact information if you want to learn more about those specific laws; please do not rely on this book to give you a complete and thorough understanding of the law or the criminal justice system!

None of the names I have used throughout this book are real names. The events are.

PART 1

TRAINING SCHOOL

CHAPTER 1
PROUD

I didn't grow up wanting to be a police officer, particularly. There aren't family photos tucked away of me in a kid's police officer costume arresting my parents or giving my teddy bears parking tickets. I first decided I wanted to be a police officer, and specifically a detective, at university. I had studied Criminology, and on my course there had been lots of staff who were retired police officers. They talked about it so passionately, and with such love for the job, that I was hooked; it was all I wanted to do. I was excited at the idea of doing a job that's so important, where you need skills and knowledge to gather evidence, piece things together, and solve cases. I wanted to be able to support people in what may be the worst moments of their lives. It seemed like an endlessly exciting and rewarding job to me.

I started applying for jobs after uni, but I confess that I didn't get in straight away. In fact, I failed a few applications. Eventually, the Detective Constable Degree Holder Entry Programme, or DC DHEP, came up on my radar.

The DC DHEP had always been controversial – every time I saw an application posted on social media, it was closely followed by a stream of negative comments. It was controversial because many officers believed that it was wrong to recruit people directly as a detective. Before the scheme, the role of detective was previously reserved for officers who had proven they could handle policing the streets in uniform and had passed that baptism of fire. The thought that a bunch of us would pretty much completely skip that uniform policing phase (we would only do a brief period in uniform), caused disagreement at best and bitterness at worst among many officers. They seemed to believe that, because they were made to suffer the rigours of uniform policing before being allowed to progress to being a detective, everyone else should have to as well.

The reality, though, was that there was an enormous shortage of detectives nationwide. The direct entry scheme was seen by those in charge as a solution to the crushing understaffing levels faced by investigation departments. And I can see where they are coming from. Detective work involves a different set of skills to uniform policing, and is a very different style of work. If you're more interested in the blue lights runs and intermittent adrenaline rushes of the uniform branch, the notion of sitting at a desk for long hours filling out court files and so on might not appeal. So there's no guarantee that a uniformed officer will enjoy being a detective – or have the right skills for the job. That might have been part of the reason that investigation departments were struggling with internal recruitment and retention so much.

The divisiveness of the scheme didn't bother me. I wanted to be a detective, and this was a way to do it – and do it faster than if I joined the police as a uniformed officer.

My previous applications had given me a better idea of what the interviewers would be looking for this time around. In the name of fairness, the application process is full of tickboxes and bureaucracy; I now had a better idea of which boxes to tick and how to provide answers in the right format. The STAR method of answering questions was second nature to me by now. STAR stands for "Situation, Task, Action, Result", and is a way to structure an answer to any behavioural question ("give an example of a time you did X.") Armed with this and my previous experience of the process, I passed the Thames Valley Assessment Centre with flying colours and was accepted on to their Direct Entry Detective Training scheme, after which I would be stationed in Slough as part of Thames Valley Police (TVP).

I remember my first day quite well. I drove through the picturesque rural setting of the Thames Valley Police Training Centre in Sulhamstead, and parked up thinking to myself 'this is it. My first day as a police officer.'

I met my fellow recruits, who I would spend the next 19 weeks with doing my basic training. There were just under 20 of us on the course, most in their late 20s to early 30s – though there were a couple of older women on the course as well. I was pleased to see that we were pretty evenly split, gender-wise. And, of course, we were all nervous, excited, and keen to make a great impression on our trainers and each other. We'd all picked our smartest outfits for that first day.

As the day got underway, we were ushered into a large hall in the main building, where we received talks from high-ranking officers who told us about Thames Valley Police and the history of UK policing. They also frequently expressed how special we were as detective recruits and how much they believed in this relatively new scheme. Their goal, I think, was to get us as enthused and excited as possible about the career we'd chosen. It definitely worked on me.

The following day we got back into formal wear, ready for our attestation ceremony, where we would be officially inaugurated as police officers. We all lined up in the main hall of the training centre and started practicing the lines of the Attestation oath, led by our main trainer Jessica. She was pacing up and down in front of us, making sure we were all in the right position and speaking at the right volume.

"Take your lanyards off," she said to us, "you look tidier without them."

I remember thinking that she had the definite air of a schoolteacher. Later, I realised that many of the recruits who go through Sulhamstead were between 18 and 20 years old, so the schoolteacher attitude made more sense.

Practice completed, the Magistrate and other officials came in and we went through the oaths line by line:

I (name) ...of (station and county)... do solemnly and sincerely declare and affirm that I will well and truly serve the Queen in the office of constable, with fairness, integrity, diligence and impartiality, upholding fundamental human rights and according equal respect to all people; and that I will, to the best of my power, cause the peace to be kept and preserved and prevent all offences against people and property; and that while I continue to hold the said office I will to the best of my skill and knowledge discharge all the duties thereof faithfully according to law.

It felt momentous and special, but also surreal taking an oath to serve the monarch. Afterwards we each went up to the front to receive our certificates from one of the magistrates, and were congratulated, and that was it – we were officially police officers.

Suddenly, I had all the powers of a constable. I could arrest people, or stop and search them. Or both, I suppose. Even though I had the badge to prove it, I confess that I didn't feel like a police officer. On reflection, that was hardly surprising. I hadn't done any training yet. But I remember feeling the excitement, anticipation and pride of what was to come. It was thrilling.

We received our uniforms after our attestation ceremony, and putting it on for the first time, in my small bedroom at the training centre, felt great. Even though I had absolutely no idea how to wear everything properly, or how to set up the kit belt. To my surprise, nobody explained how to wear the uniform properly – and this became one of the first hot topics of the WhatsApp group chat for our cohort. Pictures were flying back and forth that day as we all posed in our uniforms, puzzled out the kit belt, and showed off proud pictures in uniform with family and friends. It felt like a great beginning of this new chapter of our lives; it felt like becoming part of the police family.

CHAPTER 2
SULLY

Sulhamstead is located in West Berkshire. Other than being the home of the Thames Valley Police training centre, it's a small rural village between Reading and Thatcham. The training centre borrows its name from the village and is usually referred to as 'Sully' for short by everyone who knows it. It's where most recruits in TVP do their initial training to become police officers, and some of the assessments take place there as well. As we settled into Sully and got stuck into our training, my fellow course mates and I started to get familiar with the layout of the training centre. And, since you're here, I thought I might as well give you the tour.

Sulhamstead is a very tranquil place. Bunnies and squirrels were a frequent sight hopping around by the car park and accommodation sites. The fields are very green, the air very fresh. Behind the main training complex, there are several houses. Some are used for training purposes – practicing house searches, forced entry, or other scenarios – and some are inhabited by officers or trainers who work on site. I even heard about some trainers getting offered those houses on a temporary basis when they were going through a divorce.

The first building you encounter at Sully is called the 'White House'. It's immediately clear why – it looks very much like the one in Washington DC. The inside is covered in dark wood and old paintings, and tucked in the corner is a little museum too that I never actually saw open and so never got the chance to visit while I was there. Several of the rooms contain large bookcases with old police books. I remember we picked up and opened some of the books during one of our lessons. The text was incredibly poetic, but most of the content was quite ridiculous. Multiple books from the 1930s explained why women were not reliable witnesses and more manipulative than men; the phrase 'Beware of the 'sweet' woman' was a recurring phrase. The White House didn't have many classrooms, though. It was mainly used as offices for the trainers and as the reception for the training centre.

The classrooms were almost all located in the main building, 100 metres or so from the White House. Between the main building and the White House you pass by a memorial garden on your left, which features a memorial plaque with names of all fallen officers in Thames Valley. It's a solemn place, and I remember that it made the job we'd all signed up to do seem a lot more real and scary.

Further on from the garden were a few portacabins which were also used for teaching. Behind these portacabins was the dog compound with several dogs and puppies. Sadly, we didn't have much to do with the dogs during my time at Sully. We were supposed to have a visit from the canine unit as part of our training, but for reasons I can't remember it was cancelled. We had to settle for a few interactions through the fence. At one point, one of our trainers who was also training a puppy brought one of them to his sessions with us. He was cute, but particularly out of place during a serious lecture on domestic abuse (DA).

Upon entering the main building, you see the canteen on your left. It's the type of canteen you'd probably expect in a police training centre. For a low price, you can buy fairly unhealthy food including a full English breakfast, served by hard-bitten lunch ladies who had absolutely no qualms about ordering around a few officers when needed. On the right is a large chamber called the Holdsworth Hall – that's where our attestation ceremony was held, as well as every official ceremony that took place. If you leave out the other side of the main building, you come to a path heading towards the residential block for students called Imbert Court.

Rooms in Imbert Court are available to students who live at least 20 crow miles away from the training centre, as well as staff who live far away, if they need it. Breakfast and dinner are included in your stay, and the rooms are what I would imagine budget hotels from the 1960s would look like. Everything you need is there but it's very basic: a thin mattress on a single bed, a small desk, a wardrobe, and an ensuite bathroom. I lived far enough away during training that I got allocated one of the rooms, and I must say I found it quite pleasant. Even though it was basic, it was great to have a private space to relax and work – not to mention no commute.

The main complaint I heard about the rooms in Imbert Court was the cleanliness. After a while, it became apparent that the rooms hadn't been thoroughly cleaned before we arrived, weren't going to be thoroughly cleaned while we were there, and likely weren't going to be thoroughly cleaned after we left. I'd return on Mondays after spending the weekend at home to find exactly the same spots, stains and marks that I'd noticed the week before. Frequently, we'd find other people's hair in our bathrooms or on the desks. One of the trainers who lived there routinely joked: 'how many pubes will I find on the floor of my room at Imbert court today?' One of our rooms had a dead spider hanging in the corner. At first, we assumed it would be gone by the next week, and we were mildly surprised to find it there the following Monday. As the weeks passed, we became slightly fascinated by the growing state of putrefaction of this poor spider, as he continued to be left alone by the cleaning staff.

Next to Imbert Court is the gym building. As well as containing an actual gym for officers to use, the gym building contains sports halls where officer safety training is conducted, as well as some classrooms for theory-based officer safety training lessons. The final part of Sully to mention was the firearms range. It was next to the main car park, but none of us ever went in there – it was only for firearms officers.

CHAPTER 3
TRAINING BEGINS

Our training started straight after our attestation. From the second day onwards, we wore our uniform to class every day, which felt very odd at first. The last time I was in classes was at university, where half the time nobody even checked if you'd attended, let alone whether your uniform was on correctly. Most of our classes were lectures, where we sat and listened to a teacher who was explaining a certain aspect of policing. Lessons included roads policing, safeguarding, missing people, and domestic abuse – among others. These lessons were given to all police recruits. Despite their training, detectives are police officers first and foremost, so we needed a lot of the same training and skills. It felt like a luxury to me – I was being paid to sit in a classroom and learn about topics I found really interesting. At university, I had to pay to attend.

We were also given the textbook for the NIE, or National Investigator's Exam, which we would be taking at the end of our training. Run by the College of Policing, The NIE is the standard exam for anyone in the UK training to be a police investigator. The textbook was a 3kg beast that would have made an effective doorstop, or murder weapon.

As I've alluded to already, training was quite like school. Our trainers were very strict about us being exactly on time for each class, and people were publicly chastised if they were late. You'd also be chastised if your uniform was worn slightly wrong or sloppily. I remember one time where I was sat in a class waiting for it to start, and quickly looking up the day's timetable on my phone. All of a sudden, the trainer told me sternly to put away my phone.

I managed a stammered "Oh – OK" but felt quite stunned by the attitude. I understood why the approach might be appropriate for the average recruit, many of whom had only just left secondary school or college. But most of our intake were mid-20s to early 30s, adults who were not used to being treated as such. One of my course mates remarked how strange it was afterwards. But we never complained, or gave attitude back. We were all so keen to make a good impression and fit in that we just accepted that was the way things were.

The focus on phones was nothing compared to the focus on uniforms, though. The way you wore your uniform was scrutinised in minute detail by trainers and other senior officers at the centre. If you wore your uniform wrong and a senior officer saw you, they might report back to your trainer – which would reflect badly on you and your trainer. If that happened, you could expect a telling off from your trainer.

I honestly never got the obsession with uniform, or why it seemed to be the top priority for the senior officers at Sully. Other cohorts had to do a morning uniform parade and inspection (thankfully we were spared that, though intakes after ours did eventually have to parade). Trainees lined up every morning to be inspected, and potentially publicly scolded. I'd always known that being in the police would be serious, but I'd imagined that the focus would be on working hard, knowing your stuff, and developing your skills. I'd never expected them to be more serious about the angle of our hats than our competency for the job.

Some uniform rules were intuitive when you considered that the police are highly visible in the community and your appearance would affect how the public saw you. Shirts needed to be tucked in, shoes needed to be shiny. Some rules were archaic, others simply bizarre. For example, you always had to wear your hat when outside, but you had to take it off indoors. Correct hat etiquette, I suppose, but very old-fashioned. Then we come to the woman's police hat. It's a god-awful bowler hat, and it has to be worn so that when looking from the side it's horizontal. However, wearing it that way seriously blocked your vision. I kept slightly lifting the hat so that I wouldn't have to walk around with my head tilted back to see properly and, much to my amusement, Jessica kept pulling it down again. I remember thinking that I could either wear the hat correctly and walk into lamp posts all the time, or

I could do my job properly – but not both! The men's hats did not seem to have this issue (they had a choice of two, a cap and a traditional hat, known as a custodian's helmet).

The trousers were also a source of contention for the female officers. Simply put, they were an absolutely terrible fit. Some of my course mates ended up sending their trousers back two or three times, before giving up and going with the first pair, which were the least bad option. Mine fit so poorly I couldn't lift my legs in them – not great if I was going to pursue anyone on foot. When I did my rotation in uniformed policing, I ended up buying my own trousers, just so I could work comfortably – as did many officers in the uniform teams. If that sounds a bit strange to you after reading all about the strict uniform rules, then I'll tell you now that once I got to my station I was amazed to find out that the uniform standards were completely different. For instance, no one wears hats unless they're attending an official event or going to deliver a death message. At Sully we had all this faff about wearing a hat outside and the exact position of it on your head, and then in the real world you don't even wear it.

The uniform was just one part of a definite army vibe about the place. We had to call our sergeants 'sarge' and anyone with the rank of inspector or above 'sir', 'ma'am', or 'boss'. It felt weird to me. Having done a few jobs in between university and joining up, I was more comfortable with a system where more senior employees treat you as colleagues and equals, and you treat them the same. The word 'ma'am' sounds too much like the word 'mum' for me to ever feel comfortable addressing a superior officer using it.

I can see why the police emulated the army like this, beyond doing it for the sake of tradition. There's value in training officers to carry out orders without question during complicated and high-stress scenarios where decisive action is needed quickly. But this atmosphere of obeying authority without question was in sharp contrast with both the goals of the course and the content of our classes. Where we were taught to be 'professionally curious', to think outside the box and challenge things we disagreed with. Apparently, lots of reviews of cases where things had gone badly wrong had found that people weren't thinking critically when doing their job – they were just going through the motions and processes that their training had taught them. The drive to be professionally curious was supposed to counter that, but it seemed obvious to me that the culture and the teaching materials clashed massively. Worse, I'm not sure that the senior officers ever saw the problem.

Despite the contradiction between our training and the culture at Sully, trainers would often tell the class that our cohort had a good reputation amongst the teaching staff. I was a little surprised by that. Most people in the group were keen and professional but sometimes they also fell back into school-like behaviours: focussing more on making friends than learning the class materials, disengaging during classes, being on their phones during classes, or complaining they were tired or bored. As I think about it, I believe this was at least partly triggered by the fact that trainers treated us like school children every day. Sometimes people started acting like it.

We had a lot of trainers during our 19 weeks of training, but there were three who were the main trainers for our cohort. You've already met Jessica. She was in her 50s and used to be an inspector before she moved into training. She was quite proper, and I know that some of my course-mates thought she was very stern, but I liked her and found her quite funny. For me, she struck the balance between being human and being authoritative really well. One story she told us that made me laugh a lot was the time she had to arrange for a visit from new police and crime commissioner for us. She'd been given an address to email in order to book in to see them, and she had assumed it was for the secretary. 'Hi Matt,' she'd written to him, 'please can you just book us in to see the commissioner soon' or something similar. As it turned out, it was the email for the commissioner himself, who – somewhat haughtily – replied and signed off 'regards, MATTHEW'. Her telling of the story managed to encompass recognition of her own cock-up, an acknowledgement of the funny side of it, and ever so slight overtones of disapproval at the commissioner's behaviour. It was brilliant.

There was another trainer called Amber, who was in her late 20s. She used to be a detective herself. She was knowledgeable, ambitious, and hardworking, but never seemed to display much emotion. I put it down to the fact that we were nearly the same age as her; it seemed to me that she was trying to remain distant to try and maintain some authority over us, which she felt her age alone didn't bring.

The last trainer was a guy in his 50s who we'll call Dan. Dan was a bit wacky. During one class, he said to us:

"Do you ever do online shopping while tipsy? It doesn't end well, does it?" and proceeded to show us a porcelain frog he'd bought while drunk a few days ago. Another example was the radio procedure class, where he went on and on about saying 'over' at the end of a transmission. For the rest of our training, he would always address someone with their hand up with "go ahead, over!" He was also a fan of gesturing with his thumb like Trump and Boris Johnson, something that people made fun of him for eventually. Despite all that, though, people liked Dan because he was unashamedly himself.

CHAPTER 4

WORKLOAD AND OST

As we got to know our way around Sully and got familiar with our trainers, life started to settle into a pattern. My training was fun, but it was also incredibly intense. I think it's safe to say that none of us had any kind of life while we were at Sully!

Firstly, there were the classroom sessions I've already described. They ran from 9-5 (with half an hour for lunch), five days a week. I also usually liked to type up my notes from each class afterwards, to help make sure what I was learning had gone into my brain.

Lots of our classes also had homework set – sometimes just reading ahead for the next class, or preparing something to present to the class.

We also had university sessions to do. The DC DHEP was partly a police training course, but also a university course – at the end of our two-year probation, we would receive a postgraduate certificate in Professional Policing Practice. So some weeks we'd be attending university lectures instead of practical police training. And my god, those sessions were dull. They were mostly remote, so we had entire days spent on Teams in our rooms, moving from one virtual class to the next; staying alert and engaged felt almost impossible. We also had assignments to complete for the university course, which had to be done on our own time.

There were some e-learning courses to do as well; though these were timetabled for us, the time set aside for them wasn't actually enough to get everything done – so again, evenings and weekends had to be spent getting those done.

And just in case you thought that our evenings and weekends weren't filled enough, there were the hours spent leafing through the endless pages of the NIE textbook, revising for the NIE at the end of training.

The whole class and I felt the pressure through our entire time at Sully, and evenings off were few and far between. However, because everyone was so motivated to be there, we just got on with it. And being in it together made it easier to bear than if we'd been studying alone, of course.

Another part of our training at Sully was something called Officer Safety Training (OST for short). OST was physical training which included self-defence, restraint techniques, and use of the various items in the police toolkit. Those included handcuffs, baton, PAVA spray, and leg restraints. Two of those are likely familiar to everyone but I'll quickly explain what PAVA spray and leg restraints are.

PAVA spray is the equivalent of pepper spray – an irritant spray. It's used to incapacitate someone who is resisting by temporarily blinding them and causing a strong burning pain. I'm relieved to say that we didn't have to be sprayed ourselves in order to use PAVA; having seen it in use while on shifts, it's not something I'd ever want to experience! During training exercises and scenarios, we used water – and our assailants would have to act as convincingly as possible.

Leg restraints were essentially a very strong type of Velcro which you could use to put around someone's legs if they were very resistant during arrest or restraint. Very handy to avoid being kicked while on the job.

OST sessions were the training I looked forward to the most. I've always been good at sports and physical exercise, and I enjoyed learning about the different self-defence and restraint techniques. Besides the practical scenarios, we also had some classroom-based training for OST. We learnt use of force legislation and considerations around the use of force, situational awareness, risks such positional asphyxia (restricting someone's breathing by putting them in a certain position), and conditions such as acute behavioural disorder, or ABD. ABD is worth mentioning here because it perfectly demonstrates how difficult police work can be.

Also referred to as excited delirium, ABD is a medical emergency where the person presents with delirium, severe agitation, often aggressive behaviour, and dysfunction in the nervous system that can cause rapid heart rate and breathing. Their bodies produce an enormous amount of heat which often leads to the person suffering with ABD taking their clothes off. Of course, with symptoms like that ABD patients are often intercepted by the police, and are so agitated that they may require restraint, though they may not react to usual techniques such as PAVA spray. It's known that alcohol and drug consumption, as well as pre-existing mental conditions, can bring on ABD. But beyond that, it remains a peculiar and puzzling condition.

If a police officer believes a suspect has ABD, then, they need to treat them as if they were having a medical emergency – while also trying to keep nearby members of the public and themselves safe from the person suffering with ABD. We were advised to try de-escalation where possible, but in most cases communication with the individual is impossible because they were so agitated. Unfortunately, if the person is not quickly brought to hospital ABD is likely fatal. It shows how important our training was – but also demonstrates the complexities of modern policing.

During our practical classes I discovered that handcuffing is actually harder than it looks. You have to be in the right position and place them around the suspect's wrists in a certain way, otherwise you risk twisting their arm or wrist too much. They are also fairly tricky to take off. Once you've inserted the small key in the bottom of the cuffs, you usually have to turn the key left and right a few times before they actually come off.

We also learnt that throughout the handcuffing process you have to talk the subject through what you're doing and what you want them to do: "Put your hands out to the side", "open your hands and show me your palms", "Hands on your head", and so on. Of course, this can often help suspects understand what you want from them and avoid the need for further use of force; often, in my experience, it became about proving you'd done everything right so that nobody could sue you for injuring them during an arrest or something like that.

A great example – the use of force always had to be accompanied by a clear command: 'get back!' As such, a lot of the time we were constantly shouting 'get back!' at our partners during training exercises.

We were also taught 'signal phrases' during OST. Signal phrases were about signalling your intent to colleagues: for instance, if we said to a suspect 'is there anything I can reasonably do or say to make you cooperate?' our colleagues would know that we were about to go 'hands-on'. It was supposed to be used after you had given instructions to someone and given them several opportunities to comply with these instructions, which they hadn't taken. As with many things we covered in training, no one in the real world seemed to use this phrase. Officers would just go hands-on whenever it was appropriate without using the signal phrase.

I enjoyed OST, but I couldn't help feeling that we didn't spend nearly enough time practising each technique for it to become instinctive. I felt certain that when the time came to use these skills in the real world, under pressure in a volatile situation, we would all struggle. Any physical activity, but especially self-defence techniques, need to very nearly become muscle memory for you to be able to quickly and correctly deploy them under stress. But we only practiced defending ourselves against a knife attack for about 20 minutes – hardly enough time to fully learn the moves.

By the end of most days, I had already forgotten how some of the moves I had learnt were done. I went to the OST trainer and asked if he had ever considered making videos of the techniques and uploading them to the training platform so that people could re-watch them in their own time. After all, the only way we'd ever be able to get good enough at these moves was constant practice.

"We have videos," he replied, "but they're not available on the website right now. They will be up soon."

The videos were still not available by the time I'd finished my training at Sully. I noticed during my training that when I talked to the trainers about creating helpful tools for students I'd get one of two answers. It was either a resigned answer like 'Yes, we tried that', or an answer meant to reassure us: 'Don't worry. You'll learn that when you are at your station.'

That was a common response in every class – sometimes it felt like most of the things I wanted to know would be revealed once I had actually finished my training. It didn't sit very well with me. I'm the kind of person who wants to be as prepared as possible before I get out into the real world.

Especially for a job as important and risky as being a police officer. But most of the times when I tried to clarify my understanding, during or after class, I got the same response: 'don't worry about it – you'll learn that soon enough at your station.'

It turned out that none of our training really prepared us for the first weeks in uniform on the streets, anyway. But we'll get to all that in good time.

CHAPTER 5

FIRST OP DAY

After seven weeks of training, we were ready for our first operation, or 'op day'. This was a whole day of role plays designed to test our knowledge and skills. So far, we had learnt about powers of arrest, stop and search, writing in our pocket notebook, radio procedure, and writing statements – on top of the OST training which had included self-defence, restraining suspects, using our baton and PAVA spray, and dealing with edged weaponry. Now was the time to put our skills and knowledge to the test.

True to form for Sully, op days were also a time to make sure our uniform was perfect. We all had to wear high visibility jackets; some people even had to wear high visibility trousers. To this day I'm not sure why, as during everyday policing you usually only wear high vis jackets and trousers when policing the roads. But we all made an extra effort to look sharp. Our shoes were polished, our hair was tightly pulled back, our hats horizontal.

Everyone was nervous, including me. I felt like my training was going well – but the op day was an unknown, and that put me on edge. Op days definitely felt like they could be pivotal moments where you'd suddenly discover you are awful at being a police officer, and I am sure everyone felt under pressure to perform and show their worth as an officer. I was determined to do my best – and not to be too hard on myself if I didn't do that well.

We were each partnered with a classmate and we'd patrol around the training centre. I was paired with a girl from our group we'll call Nadine who I really liked. She was funny and warm, but serious when it came to work. During our patrols, we would be called up on the radio by a trainer playing the role of dispatch, who would send us to a 'job'. We needed to ask for some more relevant details from 'dispatch' and then state to the trainer over the radio that we were '05' or 'code 5', meaning we were on the way to the location. At each job an assessor was present, who after we had dealt with the scenario would give us feedback.

One of our jobs was to respond to a report that a suspicious man has been seen looking into cars and feeling door handles at the White House. Another was that someone had just called and said they'd been burgled, and we needed to attend. We also had a neighbour dispute in which one neighbour punched the other, and I arrested him. Nadine arrested a burglary suspect while I spoke with the victim. It was all very exciting, though a little unrealistic at times because the majority of the role players were elderly people. I have no idea where Sully found them or what they did when they weren't pretending to be burglars or angry neighbours.

Finally, there was an OST scenario. Dispatch called us to say that someone was unwell at the gym, but didn't give us much more information. Nadine and I looked at each other. If it was in the gym, we knew things were going to get physical.

We tentatively entered the gym, in which a house had been built of big foam blocks. It was quiet. We knocked on one of the foam pads which represented the front door.

No answer.

"Police, open the door!" one of us called. Still no answer.

We decided to force entry. Thankfully we didn't have to batter down the door – it opened and we entered the house with our PAVA and batons drawn. My heart was racing. The narrow black corridors created by the foam pads were menacing; it was the kind of place where someone could jump out at you at any minute.

Nadine opened the next door down the corridor. The room was empty – but several big knives were lying on the floor.

"What shall we do with these?" said Nadine. We hadn't covered what to do in this situation in our training.

"Erm, let's seize them and put them in the car" I said, improvising.

We continued to the next room. I opened the door and immediately saw a man kneeling on the floor, hunched over. He was motionless and silent.

"Sir, are you OK?" I tried.

No response. But I spotted a large knife lying on the floor between the man and myself.

What the hell was I supposed to do? This was totally outside my knowledge and certainly my experience. I had no idea what state of mind the man was in, but his complete lack of response and strange position were unnerving.

I decided to shuffle forward slightly and kick the knife out of the man's reach. As soon as I kicked the knife, the man jumped up from his kneeling position, towards me, with a knife in his hand. I immediately raised my baton – but even as I did, I realised that if this had been real, I would have most definitely been stabbed.

"End of scenario!" The assessor shouted. Needless to say, Nadine and I did not pass that scenario.

Once we were outside the house again, the assessor explained that this scenario was designed to trip people up – but that students usually learnt a lot from their mistakes. They explained how Nadine and I should have positioned ourselves in the house: we should always have eyes on our exit route and each other. Given the presence of so many knives in the house, the assessor advised that we shouldn't have approached the man straight away. Plus, I could see from where I was that he was breathing and there was no sign of injuries, so he wasn't in need of any emergency treatment. We'd have been much better off providing information over the radio while staying at a distance, keeping an eye on each other and our exit route.

It was a lightbulb moment for both of us. There will always be situations that fall outside your training and your expertise, and in those moments your first instincts aren't always going to steer you in the right direction. I appreciated the lesson, but others on the course thought it was unfair to set us up to fail.

Unfortunately, we never got the chance to drill a similar scenario again. There were four op days throughout training, but these contained different scenarios and there just wasn't time to revisit it.

At the end of the op day everyone gathered back in the classroom. We were exhausted but elated at having completed our first op day, at having come as close as possible to the real world of policing. Everyone was laughing and exchanging stories of the role plays. One of our trainers, Dan, spoke to us.

"Well done, everyone. I know the first op day is dauting, but you all did very well". I looked around; everyone was glowing with relief and excitement.

"Unfortunately…", Dan continued, "I have also had some negative feedback from the Inspector".

Everyone looked confused. We'd never met the Inspector at Sully; we didn't even know who they were. Dan continued,

"He observed some of you during the op day and said you looked, in his words, like…. 'sacks of shit'."

At first, I thought he was joking. As I looked at Dan's face, the relief I felt at having got through the op day faded and was replaced with feeling completely gobsmacked. Everyone had taken extra care to look as smart as possible for the first op day. What could possibly have been wrong?! Everyone else was in a similar state of confusion and indignation, and we demanded to know why and what we'd done wrong.

Apparently, some of the girls did not pull their hair back tightly enough, and some of our hats were slightly lopsided on our heads. That was it.

I still can't believe that this was the only feedback we got from the Inspector. He had nothing to say about our attitude during the role plays, or about our knowledge. Sat in that room, I suddenly remembered that a senior officer had been watching one of my scenarios. I saw him out of the corner of my eye, but I was too focused on dealing with the scenario to pay attention to who he was or notice his rank. At the end of the scenario, the assessor asked him whether he'd had any feedback to contribute. He brusquely said "No" and walked away.

At least, I hoped, that meant my uniform had been up to scratch. Though, from the reactions of my course mates, nobody else had been pulled up on their uniform in the moment – so the Inspector had obviously waited until afterwards to share that bit of feedback. Which, assuming that was the case, said to me that the Inspector was far more interested in criticising us than in smart uniforms – otherwise, why didn't he say anything in the moment?

Having been through the system, I don't think this is the best way to instruct and shape new police officers – whether they're detectives or uniformed officers. The obsession with the uniform, the public scoldings for lateness, the faceless inspector who didn't deign to comment on anything about our training apart from to say that we looked like sacks of shit – it all felt like a power play.

I won't say that outward appearances like uniform and timeliness aren't important in police work – of course they are. But at Sully I didn't feel like there was any connection made between those things and their actual purpose in the real world. It all felt like excuses for the top brass to show off their superiority, to demonstrate to us that they were in charge and had absolute power over us, down to the angle of our hats. It felt like an attempt to institutionalise us.

CHAPTER 6

SPECIALIST UNITS AND THE BLACK WALL SCENARIO

The rest of our training continued in much the same vein as I've just described to you. The classes filled our minds with masses of detail that we needed to learn about policing, our OST classes took us through physical defence and restraint techniques at lightning speed, op days kept us on our toes, and our evenings and weekends were swallowed by coursework, e-learning, and NIE revision. We also had one day of first aid training, which to my surprise was basically the same as any other workplace first aid course. I'd expected that we'd do a lot more first aid than that.

Despite the occasional power play politics and the intense pace, I was enjoying myself – except for the university sessions.

Far more interesting for us were the visits from the various specialist units in TVP. Ostensibly they were designed to help us learn more about the different types of policing out there, though I'm sure many of the officers who attended viewed it as a recruitment opportunity. It quickly became clear that there was a divide between 'sexy' and 'not so sexy' specialist units. Things like firearms definitely fell in the sexy category, as did the dog section. Fraud and economic crime fell in the opposite category. The investigators that came to speak to us from these units were more like accountants or stuffy college professors. The work they do is of course hugely valuable – but you could tell that everyone would rather be a firearms or dog officer, if given the choice.

Some of the specialist sessions were quite strange. For instance, we did a 'fast roads day'. We thought this would be one of the more exciting sessions – and we were down at the Madejski Stadium in Reading, so it was a nice change of scenery. However, we spent most of the day learning how to set up a cone taper of between 200 and 300 metres, to make an accident safe. We spent hours laying out cones in a line, and then slowly moving them further out into the "road" (in reality a bit of the Madejski Stadium car park) to slowly close off a lane. It was a very weird day.

More amusing was our 'driving day'. We'd been told when we signed up that we would not be trained to drive on blue lights as we wouldn't need to drive on blue lights as detectives. So nobody really knew what this driving course was going to be about. It was online, so we all logged in, to be greeted by a superintendent who sounded like a drill sergeant. In strident tones he started to tell us how important the driving course was, and it became apparent that he was telling us about the blue lights driving course. We all checked the window that Dan the trainer was in; he was nodding along, not aware that anything was amiss. Finally, one of the older ladies on the course plucked up the courage to raise her hand.

"What is it?" The superintendent asked.

"I'm sorry sir, it's just… we don't know why we're on this course. We were told we wouldn't be trained to drive on blue lights."

"Really?"

"Yes, sir."

"Dan!"

"Yes, sir?" Dan piped up from his corner of the screen.

"What the hell am I doing here?"

"Uh…"

"Why are you wasting my time, Dan?"

"Well… um…"

We watched Dan splutter his way through another few minutes of conversation, before the Superintendent abruptly ended the lesson and left the call.

Given that the detective course was still relatively new, I suppose errors like this were pretty understandable – but the exchange with Dan was really quite funny. Luckily Dan had a good sense of humour and could laugh with us at his own misfortune afterwards.

Not long after that, we had our final OST training. In our calendars, it was called "Black Wall Scenario," which was as intriguing as it was ominous. It was a solo scenario, and we were given no briefing other than being told that we'd be using our batons, PAVA spray, and self-defence techniques.

On the day, the instructor also showed us a rubber knife.

"This will form part of the scenario," he said, "but it's not just rubber."

He clicked a button on the side of the knife, and we heard the zap of an electric current surging through the knife. I felt my adrenaline jump up a notch.

"Who wants to go first?" the trainer said.

My hand shot up. I did not want to spend any more time waiting and thinking about the electric shock knife than I had to. Another girl's hand shot up too, and I ended up going second – good enough.

The first girl went in. Waiting in the hallway outside the gym, we couldn't hear much. There were a few loud shouts, and after what felt like only a few minutes it was over. Next up, me. I entered the gym to find the big foam, cushioned blocks set up like a house.

"Scenario live!"

Shouted the trainer as he closed the door behind me. The big, black blocks loomed beside me. Because of the way the blocks were made – and the fact that I was in a house – any of them could actually be a door, instead of a wall. I had no way of telling which angle someone could approach, or attack, me from. I stood there, assessing the situation.

I didn't have long to wait.

It was only a few seconds into the scenario when someone burst through one of the walls, shouting abuse and charging at me. I'm proud to say that I didn't feel any fear – just a wave of adrenaline surging through me.

"GET BACK!" I shouted and pushed him off me. Before he could come at me again, I grabbed my PAVA spray, took aim, and sprayed. A few seconds later he went down screaming in pain.

Seconds later I heard the zap of the knife – behind me. I turned around just in time to block the stab of the knife with my hand. I deployed my spray again and incapacitated the second assailant.

"Good" the assessor said from the corner of the room where they'd been watching. "Now move on to the next room." They indicated one of the blocks that I was supposed to go through.

Heart pounding, I proceeded to the next room.

"You have to arrest the suspect and use your baton," said the trainer.

I saw the actor in the middle of the room, holding a big foam pad to the side of his body. That was a familiar sight; all through our training, every time we'd done baton work, we'd be in pairs. One of us would hold the pad over a part of our body, and the other would hit it.

The moment the man saw me, he became aggressive. He began cursing, shouting, and walking quickly towards me in an aggressive manner. I drew my baton and shouted,

"Get back!"

The subject only became more agitated. He ignored my demand and continued advancing. The moment he came within my personal space, I wacked his leg with the baton on the pad he was holding. He shouted out in pain and backed off.

"GET ON THE FLOOR NOW!" I shouted.

"FUCK YOU!" he roared, charging at me again with his fist raised.

I struck again with my baton. He fell on the floor grabbing his leg and shouting in pain.

"STAY DOWN! PUT YOUR ARMS OUT TO THE SIDE!" I yelled. The subject finally complied, though he was still swearing and cursing. I handcuffed him and looked at the assessor.

"End of scenario," he said.

He gave me some points of feedback – most importantly that I'd let go of my baton while cuffing the suspect, inadvertently creating an opportunity for someone to steal my weapon. I'd done this because the baton I'd been given for the duration of my training at Sully was a bit broken and very difficult to retract. Not that I'm making an excuse – after all, there was no guarantee that I'd get a fully working baton once I was in the real world. Despite this, I passed! I was thrilled!

Most of the class passed the first time. Two or three had to take the test again a few weeks later, including the girl who went before me. Looking back, I suspect that the pass or fail was just as much about your reaction as it was about following procedures properly. The scenario was designed to test how you reacted to a scary situation, see if you could hold your ground in the face of physical and verbal aggression, and see if you could still put the OST techniques you'd learned into practice under those conditions.

And that was the end of my OST at Sully. Just like with the specialist unit visits, a few elements got cancelled for reasons that were never explained. We were supposed to have a public order training day that never happened, as well as a training scenario in a fist suit. I was disappointed about that one. A fist suit is a full protective suit that allows you to receive punches, kicks and blows with a baton without getting hurt – the training was about using your baton and restraining a person. I didn't want to miss part of basic training and feel behind straight away – but there wasn't really any choice.

Thankfully, I did get to do the fist suit scenarios at a later stage during my time in the police. We got a one-day OST refresher once a year; during my refresher I did a scenario with a fist suit. It was actually so much fun.

CHAPTER 7

FIREARMS AND PASSING OUT

One of the last specialist sessions we had at the training school was firearms. We weren't sure what to expect, but four of us had been asked to bring their stab vests along, including me. So everyone was a bit nervous about what was going to happen at the session. As I said, most of our training was done in classrooms on PowerPoint; you didn't need a stab vest for a PowerPoint presentation.

When we walked in and took our seats there were two very muscley officers standing at the front of the classroom, and several types of firearms laid out on the table. The two officers honestly looked like they'd just stepped out of an action movie. They were ripped, they looked tough, and they were decked out in their specialist uniforms. They captured the attention of everyone in the room far better than any PowerPoint.

The two officers started out by explaining what the role of firearms officer was all about, and they asked if anyone had ever considered the role. Quite a few hands went up; I got the impression that some people had decided just this second that being a firearms officer was something they'd like to consider quite seriously.

After the initial talk, we were allowed to pick up the guns to get a feel for them. They were real weapons – though obviously unloaded. Everyone rushed to the front and started picking up various guns, aiming them at the far wall. After everyone had tried holding the guns we moved on to the next part of the training session.

"We've got a scenario planned for you," said the first officer.

"Who volunteered to bring their body armour?" asked the second. I hesitantly put up my hand as did three other students. "Put them on and put these on as well," he said, handing the four of us ear protectors. All I could think was: 'what the hell is going to happen?'

The scenario began, and we received a briefing. We were told our call sign, our shift, and the details of a job we would be attending. A man had been seen acting aggressively outside his ex-partner's address and was reported to have a gun.

"On your way," said the first officer.

I was partnered with a guy from my class – let's call him Jared – that I clicked well with. Jared was ex-army and so quite familiar with firearms already; I knew he would be keen to join the unit.

With the rest of the class watching, Jared and I approached the scene outside. The 'ex-partner's' address was at one of the houses at the edge of the training centre. As we approached, I heard a man shouting aggressively. I was just standing around the corner of the hedge of the neighbouring house.

"Wait before we approach," said Jared. "Let's try and see whether he actually has a gun first."

I carefully peeked around the corner of the hedge and saw the guy, still shouting frantically and waving his arms.

"I can't see one," I told Jared. I turned my head back and looked again.

It was of course at that moment that the man pulled out a handgun and started firing into the sky. Then, he looked in my direction and made eye contact with me.

"RUN!" I yelled to Jared, and we took cover behind the bricks of the neighbouring house while we called for backup on the radio. With our backs against the wall of the house, we had lost sight of the male with the gun. We realised that he could approach us from either side of the house, at any moment.

We stood stock-still for about 20 seconds.

Suddenly, someone walked around the corner, and we jumped up. It was the trainer.

"End of scenario," he said, smiling.

Back in the classroom we were interrogated as though we were in court.

"Which hand was he holding the gun in?"

"What exactly did the man say?"

"What colour were his trousers?"

I didn't know the answer to any of the questions. I'd just been worried about the gun and staying alive. My colleague couldn't recall any more detail either.

"This is an illustration of how difficult it is to be a firearms officer," one of the officers explained. I got the point. If you're a firearms officer, the pressure on you is enormous. You have to make split-second decisions that could lead to a victim – or the suspect – suffering life-changing injuries or death, while putting your own life in danger. And after all that, the justice system and the public expect them to recall every detail. That's just not how human brains work. Yet, the media and the public feel perfectly comfortable sharing their thoughts or judgements on the actions of officers in these situations. Among police officers these people were often referred to as the 9am jury, because they waited until they had had a full night of sleep and had thoroughly considered the situation before passing judgement, believing that the officers should have come to the same conclusion in the heat of the moment.

Suddenly everyone had forgotten about their ambition of becoming a detective and was buzzing about the prospect of becoming a firearms officer. Sensing this, our main trainers were suddenly keen to get rid of the two firearms guys.

"No, no, they are going to be detectives," Jessica said in her smiling but serious way as she thanked them for their time and ushered them out of the room. Once they'd gone, she turned to us and said: "all specialist units will be open to you…after you've finished your detective training."

Despite the buzz, though, I wasn't tempted to join the firearms team. While I know that every role in the police helps keep people safe in some way, I didn't want to do it with a gun in my hand. Just my personal choice.

After the firearms visit, there really wasn't much left of our course. We'd submitted all our coursework, we had our final reviews, and we had a passing out ceremony in full uniform where we got our certificates. And one week after everything else had finished, we took the NIE. It was one of the hardest exams I've ever done. Two hours of multiple-choice questions, though the volume of questions meant you had to move through them at breakneck speed, desperately trying to recall as much of the leviathan NIE textbook sat back in our rooms. Thanks to the sacrificed evenings and weekends, I'm pleased to say that I passed, along with the majority of our cohort. Two people failed; they were allowed one retake – if they failed that, they would be kicked off the course. Thankfully, they passed the second time.

I felt incredibly proud to have completed my training. It was intense, some of it was confusing at times, but I'd done it – I was on my way to becoming a full-fledged police detective.

Everyone on the course was emotional. We'd been through so much together, learned so much, and relied on each other for support – both with classwork and the strain of training. There were a lot of group selfies taken, pictures with best friends, and someone even made a slideshow with as many photos as they could find from our training. A number of us went to the pub afterwards to celebrate. Much like any graduation, we were all caught up in the intensity of the moment, confident that we would be firm friends forever.

Sadly, our group chat is now pretty much completely defunct. Because, like any graduation, your life afterwards whisks you off in a variety of different directions. One of our OST trainers, pretty bluntly, told us at our graduation:

"Yeah, I felt the same way with my training class. You're never going to see each other again."

And he was right. At least, we were never all in the same room again. Though some of us managed to meet up in ones and twos. We all went to different stations, with different shift patterns, and – naturally – started to forge relationships with our new colleagues. Some of us dropped out, some sooner and some later. And others fell out over things, the way friends do. But none of that takes away from the wonderful memories we made at Sully, and the experience we went through. My classmates were brilliant, and they helped me face the next phase of our policing career with enthusiasm and excitement.

PART 2
ICR

CHAPTER 8

WELCOME TO SLOUGH

Before ever setting foot in Slough, I knew it had a bad reputation. At Sully, everyone who I told where I was going to be based reacted with "ooh, good luck," or "oh, that's gonna be busy," or they'd just wince. Slough was considered the 'worst' or busiest area of Thames Valley, both in terms of the volume of crime and in the seriousness of the crimes committed.

To add to the picture being painted in my head, I'd had a meeting with my new tutor, Jay, before my first shift. He told me that officers were strongly advised not to arrive or leave work in their 'blacks' – the trousers and T-shirt that officers wear under their vests – due to the risk of being recognised and attacked by the public.

I suppose that would have freaked out some people, but honestly the excitement of finally being able to start frontline police work overrode any unease I might have felt about the risk of being attacked on my commute. And the ritual of changing into and out of uniform helped to create a bit of a divide between work and personal life. I arrived as a civilian, changed into my uniform, and the chaos of the job began. At the end of a shift, I'd change back into my clothes and leave the job behind. At least, that's how it went for a while.

So, full of excitement, nerves, and determination, with 19 weeks of training at Sully under my belt, it was time for my first shift. A 5am start had me standing outside the police station at 6:30am, ready and raring for my 7am shift to start.

I hadn't received any instructions about where to go or who to find when I first got to the station. I'd been hoping to bump into my tutor before too long and rely on them to help me get my bearings, but in the end I asked a PC I met in the stairwell where I could get changed. The answer, as it turned out, was in the upstairs toilets. Given that advice about not arriving in uniform, it struck me as odd that we had nowhere to get changed – but I shrugged it off. Perhaps this lack of a changing place was also the reason why I can't remember seeing anyone get changed at all at the station.

Uniform on, I headed back downstairs and finally bumped into my tutor, Jay.

I've mentioned my tutor a few times now, so I'll take a moment to explain their role in a new PC's job. When they first arrive at their station, every new officer is assigned a tutor, who is a more experienced police officer. They're in charge of assessing you in your first ten weeks on the job and supporting you in your first two years. That includes making sure you've been to enough different types of incidents, checking you followed the right procedures at those incidents, and have generally learned the role of being a police officer. As we'd be doing rotations in different departments across our two years, DC DHEP members like me would have a variety of tutors across those two years – though I soon learned that didn't always happen. My first tutor, Jay, was great. He was confident, kind, and seemed genuinely interested in helping me settle in. He was also never afraid to wear his blacks in public on the way to or from work.

We followed everyone else into the briefing room for my first briefing, and sat down to a slide show of the faces and details of wanted people and outstanding actions for us to complete. Later on, I started to recognise the recurring faces and details in briefings and they got much easier to follow – but on that day I can safely say that the information came at me so fast that afterwards I could recall none of it.

I do remember very clearly, though, that at one point in the briefing, one of the sergeants said:

"Who's dealing with that rape?"

The other sergeant replied:

"Which one?"

And, to my complete surprise and discomfort, everyone started laughing.

I want to be clear here that I am not suggesting that my colleagues were uncaring or unprofessional about the crimes we were discussing. I wasn't surprised because I thought they didn't care; I was surprised that everyone was so relaxed about these crimes. At Sully we had sat through lectures and training about how impactful rapes are, how important it is to treat the victim with respect, and the seriousness of the crime – yet here in the real world it was an everyday occurrence, something that could be laughed about in a briefing. It felt so inappropriate. I had assumed that the attitudes drilled into me at Sully were representative of the rest of the police. The reality was quite different; to say I felt like a fish out of water would have been an understatement.

There was no special mention made of me at the briefing. A sergeant found me after the briefing, said "welcome", and explained that my 'main' sergeant (and line manager) was on holiday that week. Their tone made it clear that they were neither particularly interested nor excited about my joining.

I didn't react. I'd learned early on that confidence was everything in the police. We needed to radiate confidence to the public and to suspects and victims we interacted with; building that confidence started inside the station. So, despite feeling like I had landed on an alien planet, with my ideas of what working for the police was like rapidly crumbling around me, I ignored the apathetic welcome and got on with my shift.

My first rotation at Slough was with the Incident Crime Response team, or ICR. The ICR teams are the uniformed officers that respond to emergencies from 999 calls and other 'live' incidents. ICR is about as frontline as you can get in the police, and teams work in 6-day shift patterns. We worked two early shifts (07:00–16:00), two late shifts (14:00–22:00), two night shifts (22:00–07:00), and then four days off. My first shift was an early – and it was busy. About ten minutes after the briefing finished, Jay and another officer were called to a mental health incident near the station. Since Jay was my tutor, I went with him.

While Jay drove, I frantically wrote down the report details in my pocket notebook as they were relayed to us over the radio. It was what we'd been taught in training – and, a bit like a drowning person clinging to a lifeline, I was convinced that if I stuck to my training I'd be OK. I looked up to see Jay smiling.

"What are you writing down?" he asked.

"The report details – name of the man, the address, reason for the call, that stuff." I replied. Jay laughed.

"OK," he said, amusement in his voice. It couldn't be more obvious that he was humouring me, the green new recruit, confident that my naivety would wear off in time. I soon found out that no one actually writes in their pocket notebook unless it's to record a significant statement after arrest and caution.

I kept writing, feeling my lifeline falling away from me.

We arrived at the address, which was a supported housing establishment – basically a form of assisted living for individuals with additional needs. We went up to the room, Jay knocked on the door, opened it (it was unlocked), and walked in. The strangeness of just walking into another person's home and telling them what to do stayed with me for a while.

The room was small, with no colour or decorations that I could see. Sitting on the bed we found a small Asian man in his 60s. He barely responded to Jay and the other officer, other than to say he wanted to kill himself because he had no one anymore. Jay checked the medication on the table and asked the man how much he had taken: two tablets, as prescribed.

All we could do for the man was ask him if he wanted to come to hospital voluntarily for an assessment. The police do have the power to detain someone if they are a risk to themselves or others – but only if they are in a public place, in which case you can take them to a place of safety. Thankfully, our man agreed to be driven into hospital; if he hadn't, we would have left him to it. I did hear stories that in days gone by a (frowned upon) tactic with individuals who were reluctant to accept help was to convince them to step outside, where they could be detained; as it was, we got the best outcome we could for the man. While the other officer drove him to the hospital, Jay and I returned to the station to set up my locker, keys, and other kit.

After a cup of tea and some admin – both for the job and for me as a new starter – Jay and I went out on patrol. That meant we drove around the local area, waiting for a call to come in and looking for anything that might need our attention. Despite my determination to be confident and cope, I was very anxious all day. It was my first proper day on the job that I had been working towards for years, and the pressure to perform, combined with the stakes that are often at play in police work and the complete culture shock of the day so far were taking their toll. My mouth was so dry that I struggled to speak and I had to keep sipping water. Jay spent the day gently poking fun at me and reassuring me that I was going to be fine. Jay's banter helped me calm down and get through the day – and many of the days afterwards.

Later, we got a call that a stolen motor vehicle (SMV for short) had pinged on an automatic number plate recognition (ANPR) system nearby. Jay's face lit up and he switched on the blue lights, excited about the possible pursuit. He was one of those officers who was pretty jaded – unless it came to the dangerous stuff. The more dangerous the call, the more interested he was.

We set off to see if we could find the SMV, and I was soon lost in a world of codes, acronyms and jargon that I didn't understand as we talked to the other police vehicles out looking for the SMV with us. To me it was a very confusing blur, since we'd never been trained in advanced driving.

Much to Jay's disappointment, the car had been stopped by the roads policing unit by the time we arrived. Two women in their twenties were in the front, who – as it turned out – were also suspects in a recent violent robbery in a shopping centre. In the back of the vehicle there were three children.

Jay asked me to get the names of the children for a social services referral. Since we were arresting both of the adults who were with them, social services would have to try and find a suitable relative to come and collect the children and look after them until the adults had been released from custody.

I recall that I didn't spend any time dwelling on the sadness of the situation (though it definitely was sad for those kids). I've always wanted to feel like I know what I'm doing professionally; that drive to get it right helped me to focus on the job at hand. Combined with my own talent for compartmentalisation, that usually keeps me from dwelling on the details of a job. Though speaking of details, taking names ultimately turned out to be futile – the women had given us false names for themselves and the children.

Roadside work done, we left the children with the roads policing unit and took the women to be booked into custody – one in the car with us, and the other following in another police vehicle. The woman in our car was very talkative, chatting with Jay about her life, her council house, and other details I can't remember now. I soon discovered that all officers chat with compliant suspects, which felt strange to me but actually makes a lot of sense. Building rapport with a suspect often helps you keep them calm and compliant during the process of booking them into custody, heading off a lot of unpleasantness and the possible need to use force.

Later on, I said to Jay:

"I wonder how she got a council house. They are really hard to get." Jay replied:

"You know, we chat with them – but you shouldn't believe a word they say. They're criminals, after all."

The moment we arrived in custody the other woman approached me in some state of agitation. In a voice filled with urgency and panic, she told us that her friend suffers from seizures which were dangerous. I told her that would be discussed at the custody desk with the custody sergeant. I can't say for certain whether this was true or not, but I later found out that people fake illness all the time when entering custody. I was never quite sure why they did it – it's a tactic that's extremely unlikely to get you de-arrested, for instance. The police can hold someone without charge for 24 hours, but if you're ill enough to require hospital treatment, that clock pauses while you're being treated and resumes once you're back in custody. That's certainly something that most of the serious criminals know – yet even they fake illnesses. It might just be out of spite or a desire to be difficult, but I believe that it's a way for them to exert some kind of control in an environment where they've got absolutely no control.

While we were booking in the woman we transported, the custody sergeant gave the order to strip search her – her record said that she often concealed drugs. We had to make sure that they had absolutely nothing about their person that could be used to hurt themselves, including drugs.

I did the strip search with another officer, which was a very surreal experience on my first day. We'd been trained in how to strip search someone, but it had only taken up two hours, if that. The course had focused on what we had to read out to the suspect: stuff to ensure they understood what was happening and why, and instructions for the suspect to make sure the strip search was conducted in a structured manner. We also learned how to conduct the search by force if the suspect was noncompliant. But, of course, I couldn't remember any of it in the moment. Thankfully, the other officer took the lead (which, of course, was exactly why she was there).

In case you're curious, two of the golden rules when strip searching are: never touch the suspect (unless they're noncompliant), and never make them strip fully. You do top half and bottom half separately; unless they're a character out of *Now You See Me* there's no chance of them moving anything between their clothed halves during a search, and it gives them a little bit of dignity in what is a pretty undignified process. Certainly, the woman we were searching complained at the embarrassment of the situation, though I was thankful that she was compliant – and I got the distinct feeling that this wasn't her first strip search.

A little later on, the other female suspect was brought back for a strip search as well; one of the detention officers checked on her and smelled weed in her cell. Unfortunately, this woman was less compliant; she was crying her eyes out and refused to cooperate. She also told us it was a breach of her human rights and would damage her mental health. Looking back, I'm proud that I didn't let all the stress and tension put me off doing my job in that moment; I did my best to be kind, but I told her that ultimately the decision had been made that the search needed to be carried out and that decision wasn't going to be changed. I can't say that I felt sorry for her; a few hours ago she'd been committing a violent robbery. Her presence in the cell, being strip searched, was entirely her own doing.

Meanwhile, tears were still streaming down her face, and she said she wanted to speak to a lawyer first, so a phone call was arranged. This is an area where TV shows have nearly got it right. While nobody is entitled to "their phone call" to whoever they like, everyone is entitled to speak to a solicitor after being arrested, which can happen over the phone or in person. If you should ever find yourself arrested and are hoping to call your mother to tell her where you are, that call is made for you by the police – though be careful what you ask for. One of my more amusing memories from ICR was watching a custody sergeant call a suspect's mother, only for her to go absolutely ballistic over the phone. The poor suspect couldn't hear the words, but he could see the face of the custody sergeant, and hear her replies. The look on the suspect's face indicated that he was seriously considering whether he wanted to be released at all.

Anyway, the call to the lawyer took 45 minutes or so to arrange. If you've ever wondered how people can afford this time with a lawyer after an arrest, there's a pool of what's known as duty solicitors who provide free legal advice to people who have been arrested. Once someone has requested a solicitor, the duty solicitor line is called and one of the duty solicitors takes the job.

As an aside, it's probably a good idea to explain what 'lawyer' and 'solicitor' mean. A lawyer is anyone who is a licensed legal practitioner; solicitors and barristers are both types of lawyers. A solicitor is someone who provides expert legal advice and support to clients ranging from individuals to organisations; they're different to barristers, who generally appear in court, but both are lawyers. Suspects can also speak to a 'legal representative', who is not a qualified lawyer but is still qualified to give advice to people in custody – those people sometimes get called solicitors too, though technically they aren't.

But back to the story. The solicitor my suspect spoke to was sympathetic but told the woman that the police did have powers to strip search her. And thankfully, the woman finally agreed to go into the search room. Another female officer and I searched her and we soon found a small bag of marijuana in her bra. I further arrested the woman for possession of a class B drug – and in so doing, made my first ever arrest, on my first day.

Honestly, it felt a bit anticlimactic. Even after all the police training, I had still harboured some idea that my first arrest might be after some kind of foot chase, or on a dawn raid, or something suitably dramatic. I just ended up arresting someone who was already under arrest for something else! But in a way, I was glad to have got it out of the way. Once you've started work in the police all your time up until that first arrest is spent waiting for it to come – now I could focus on the rest of the job.

Not long after, we had finished up in custody and were back in the car on the way back to Slough police station.

"OK, what do we still need to do?" Jay asked me.

"Well, only the statement, really."

"Let's get it started now so we don't have to sit around at the station doing it. Now, here's what you're going to write..."

I had been trained to get as much detail as possible into a statement – but once again, Jay gently knocked away my lifeline and essentially dictated my extremely short (to my eyes, anyway) statement to me.

Back at the station, another officer reviewed my statement.

"We can't accept your statement like that," they said.

"What's wrong with it?" I asked, a ripple of disappointment rolling over me.

"We can't say that you found some marijuana. You need to call it 'green herbal matter'." They said. "What? It's marijuana," I replied.

"Yeah, but you haven't actually been able to test it."

I was bemused, more than anything. I'm no drug user, but I know what marijuana looks and smells like. But they were right, of course. Everything in policing is about building up a solid case against suspects. That's as much about not doing the *wrong* thing as much as it is about doing the *right* thing. In this case, that meant that an 'experienced officer' would write a separate statement to say that they inspected the green herbal matter that I suspected to be a Class B drug, and they identified it as cannabis.

The conversation rolled around to my arrest soon after that.

"Are you gonna tell your friends from Sully?" Jay laughed.

And of course, I did. The WhatsApp group we started up during training was still very active – everyone had their first shifts within ten days of each other, and at the time we were all sharing our stories like mad. Over time, the group would get less active as people quit, or fell out, or got absorbed in their work and started to feel closer to their colleagues than their old classmates. But for now, that group was one lifeline that nobody – not even Jay – could take away from me.

As soon as my statement was uploaded, I left and got home around 8pm. I'd like to say that there were lots of reflections and thoughts swirling through my head after my first day – you know, the kind of stuff that would make for a really good ending to a chapter – but honestly, I was fucking exhausted. I learned the hard way that you should always have snacks in your police bag – since leaving the house at 5am, I hadn't had anything to eat. There just hadn't been any time or opportunity. Skipping meals and not eating for an entire shift was, sadly, a relatively frequent occurrence.

Looking back though, I can see how brutal that first day was. Not just in terms of what actually happened – a suicidal man, two strip searches and my first arrest – but in terms of the culture shock. I hadn't been quite so naïve as to think that everything in the real world would be just like the training centre had told us it would be. But it felt like just about *every* procedure and technique we had been taught was either slightly different, tolerated, or completely ignored in the real world. And that's not to say that the police officers I worked with were wrong or doing a bad job. But the training we were given at Sully was completely divorced from the realities of police work. It would have been great to do everything the way we were taught, but there just wasn't time for most of the things we were asked to do. But, as I said, lots of those things – writing notes, going into detail, and so on – were like lifelines. There was this unspoken idea that if I could just do those things the way they were taught to me, I'd make it through. Once it was explained to me that in the real world most of those things were either pointless or impossible to fit in on the job, those lifelines were gone. I was on a stormy sea, keeping myself afloat. And, even if I felt like I had plenty of energy left to swim right now, I didn't know just how rough the water could get.

CHAPTER 9

THE POLICING FAMILY

My first day was tough, but I was happy with the way it went. I made my first arrest, I did two strip searches – I'd got stuck in and done some good policing alongside my colleagues. Not a bad start to my ten-week stint in ICR policing. As the days began to pass, however, I came to realise that ICR wasn't always the most welcoming environment.

In many ways, I felt like I was back in high school again. The culture was extremely macho, and (unsurprisingly) dominated by the men on the force. As a newcomer I immediately got a strong feeling that I could either be one of the gang or be an outcast that everyone gossiped about behind my back. And, of course, joining any such group comes at a price. There were a few, actually. We had a 'cake fine' that could be imposed for a variety of transgressions – being late, doing something wrong, and so on. Thankfully, the cake fine stayed on the friendly side of banter. It was even a way to make people feel included – being given a cake fine was a way of saying 'you did that wrong, but it's OK' and brought you closer to everyone else. Less positively, rookies were expected to make tea for the rest of the team. In most other jobs I'd had, it was the other way around: on your first day, someone would offer you a cup of tea. But here the rules were different; newcomers had to be tested and put in their place.

I remember that in my first week, an officer who I didn't know came up to me at my desk unannounced.

"Hey," he said, "we have a rule here that new people need to make tea for the rest of the team."

"Uh… I have a meeting in five minutes that I'm just leaving for," I replied, somewhat taken aback.

"Oh, OK," the officer replied, and left. He didn't even bother to introduce himself. It was so weird – like the entire point of his coming over to my desk was to try and assert his power over me.

Given how rude I found the whole thing, I decided I would not make any tea on demand for ten weeks. Thankfully for me, Jay wasn't into that whole culture, so he didn't try and get me to go along with it – and I'm happy to say that I managed to stick to my resolution.

I mentioned already that on my first day my sergeant was not on duty. She came back to work in my second week. I saw a female sergeant that I didn't recognise, so I assumed this must be her – my new sergeant, Amy. After the briefing she didn't come to see me, so when I saw her in the kitchen later in the day I put on a smile and went over.

"Hi, you must be Amy. I'm Jade, I'm new and I think you're my sergeant."

"Oh, I'm sure we'll have a chance to catch up sometime," Amy said, and she walked away.

That was the most meaningful conversation we ever had. We never caught up, had a check in, or a one-to-one meeting. In fact, Amy barely spoke to me. She did leave for a new role during my ten weeks so perhaps she wasn't really invested in her current role by the time I met her. But the interaction, and the feeling of being unwelcome that it left me with, stuck. I had worked in several other workplaces and I'd never been treated this way. Luckily, I'm sufficiently strong-willed and confident that I didn't start to think that it was my fault people were treating me this way – but that didn't make their behaviour much easier to deal with.

It was possible that some of the attitude I experienced was because of my status as a DC DHEP officer. I mentioned before that the scheme was controversial with many officers, who believed that we should have to go through the same two years in uniform that they did before being allowed to be detectives. Nobody ever said anything like that to my face, but I wonder if I was made to feel like an outsider because, to them, I *was* an outsider. A lot of my course mates from Sully told me that they definitely felt they were treated differently because they were DC DHEP officers.

Unfortunately, things didn't get much better further up the chain of command. When I started at Slough, the station commander had sent a calendar invite to all new starters for a one-to-one welcome chat. I thought that was a nice gesture – but that meeting got cancelled and rescheduled twice. With incidents happening at unpredictable times, it was understandably hard for the commander to stick to a planned schedule, so I was patient. The third time I went to his office at the scheduled appointment time, his door was open and I saw that he was already in conversation with someone in his office.

"Shall I come back later?" I said.

"I am going to have to reschedule." He replied, "can you speak to my assistant?"

I nodded but never went to speak to the assistant. It was plain to me that, nice as the thought of a welcome meeting was, it just wasn't feasible in practice. And a part of me thought that, if we were never going to manage to have this welcome chat, why bother trying to reschedule it? After all, I wasn't a commander but I was also busy – we all were. Frankly I had more urgent things to do with my day than continually reschedule welcome meetings.

Back out among the uniformed officers, as I mentioned it felt at times a lot like high school. It wasn't uncommon for the men in the team to have playfights, hitting each other with their batons or with random objects laying around the office. People would throw stuff across the desks trying to hit their mates. During one quiet night shift some officers took my hat off my desk without asking and used it as a basket to throw crumpled balls of paper in as a game. I took it back as I didn't really want my hat to be used for that (remember I was still very proud of my uniform, and had just had nineteen weeks of obsession with my hat and where it sat on my head).

"Have a little fun," they said to me, visibly annoyed.

I remember another quiet shift where a few of the team were in the office having a takeaway dinner, and one of the guys told us all a story of how he hooked up with a 'fit bird' after a party. He told the group with great excitement – and great detail – how he had vaginal, anal, and oral sex with her – in that order. The guys at the table all burst out in laughter. I felt uncomfortable and out of place in this male locker room type environment. I couldn't image this would have happened in any of the other companies I worked for in the past.

There was also a group of officers in ICR who were really nice. They were the 'non-machos', I suppose – men and women who didn't enjoy the locker room talk and machismo on display most of the time, like me. I tried to stick with them as much as I could. One of them in particular, Sam, I really gelled with: the very first time we spoke, I felt comfortable and thought to myself 'here's someone I'm going to get along with really well.'

Sam had just finished her first ten weeks as a uniformed officer, so we were both relatively new – but she had more experience than I did. She became a confidante who I could open up to about how I was really feeling during my time in the police. Having had many similar experiences, she could sympathise. Without her I'm not sure I would have lasted as long as I did in the police, and I'm pleased to say we're still in touch to this day.

And, luckily, I found that I got on great with Jay. He had a unique mix of attributes that made him a great officer, and a good tutor. I came to think of him as a bit of a 'wild west' cop; he was never afraid to break some rules, or knock some heads together (metaphorically, of course) to get a job done. I thought it surprising that Jay volunteered to be a tutor; he didn't have much patience with many of the rules, or the paperwork, and it must have been tedious for him to retrain every new recruit to correct the things that Sully taught us wrong, or that weren't practical in real life. It started to make more sense when he told me that he hadn't actually chosen to be a tutor, but rather he had been chosen and not really given a choice in the matter. Which made it all the more amazing that he seemed to enjoy sharing his experience with people like me. And boy, did Jay have a lot of experience. It made him extremely jaded; I remember that nothing ever really shocked him or put him off-balance. The things that I as a rookie found intense and stressful, he found boring and a hassle. But despite that, he dealt with the public and managed incidents very well. He was a very human guy when dealing with incidents; he'd never lead with the paperwork. I was, and still am, incredibly glad that he was my tutor.

The next two weeks on response were a whirlwind. The lengthy shifts and the constant adrenaline left me exhausted. Every job I attended with Jay felt completely different from the last one, and every time I felt afterwards that

I should have done a million things differently. I was constantly discovering paperwork that my training hadn't even mentioned existed. I was expecting to feel this way for a little bit – it was all just part of the learning curve in these intense jobs. However, I also couldn't escape the feeling that my training had left me woefully ill-prepared. The course at Sully might as well have been for a completely different role, so big was the gap between the training and reality. In my head I conceptualised them as two separate planets, lightyears apart. Their orbits meant that sometimes they were closer and sometimes further away, but they never crossed over or even got close to each other. At the training school I had done well. My feedback was positive, I knew the answers during lessons, and I felt that I had a good grasp of the material. At Slough, I felt completely lost and had to rely on colleagues to explain basic things to me all the time.

A great example of this was how to use the police IT system, called Niche. We received two lessons on Niche in the second week of training school but it did not cover most of the things we would be using it for on a day-to-day basis. When we asked about it, we were always told the same thing:

"Don't worry about it. You'll learn once you get to your station."

Yet when we got to our station, there was an expectation that we'd already been trained on how to use Niche. So, there was no formal training on how to use the system; you had to either work it out yourself, or ask someone for help. And because we used Niche for just about everything in our day-to-day work, I was relying on help from everyone to get my job done. As I said before, I expected things to be hard and to feel a bit useless in the early days of the job – but there were multiple moments like this where I felt like my training had completely let me down. And being so reliant on others for help meant that I constantly felt pressure to stay on the good side of my colleagues, even if I didn't like their behaviour.

I was also struggling with multi-tasking and retaining verbal information. I'm someone who needs to write information down or read it in order to properly retain it at the best of times, and with the exhaustion of a new job and new shift pattern, my memory was like a sieve. On top of that, our radios were crackly, which made it hard to understand what the person on the other end was saying. We had earpieces that you could use, which I tried to see if that would help me out. It did a little, but I soon discovered that once I was dealing with an incident I simply couldn't listen to the radio and deal with what was in front of me at the same time.

You can see what it's like for yourself: go and have a conversation with your friend, while listening to a song you've never heard before. Afterwards, try and write down the song lyrics and as much detail of the conversation with your friend as you can. If you manage that, great – but then ask your friend whether the conversation was any good!

Furthermore, the radio jargon that we used in the real world was completely different to what we were told at Sully. Dan the trainer had impressed on us solemnly that we must say 'over' every time we speak to make sure the other side knows the message has finished. To make his point, for the rest of his classes, we had to say 'over' once we'd finished speaking to him.

In the real world, no one did that. Saying 'over' was a like waving a big flag saying 'newbie' on it; every new officer quickly stopped doing it. Jay even told me plainly one day: "don't say 'over'."

There was also a whole lot of new radio speak to learn. One example was 'so far'. You said 'so far' to indicate that you still had more information to give but wanted to check that the person on the other end was keeping up with you. The other person would then reply 'so far' and you'd continue relaying information.

There were definitely moments when I felt quite bitter about the lack of useful training we'd been given. It felt like we'd just been thrown into a lion's den without any preparation, means to defend ourselves, or even an idea of what was coming. We'd had 19 weeks to train and be ready, but we weren't. We deserved better as employees, but so too did the public. After all, if you've just been through a traumatic incident and need support, you want the person helping you to actually know what they're doing, right?

There's an incident I remember quite well that really summed up where I was during my first few weeks in ICR. It was a night shift, and Jay and I joined the search for a high-risk missing person (or 'misper' to use the lingo). The misper had left a note at his girlfriend's address saying that he was going to kill himself – and due to that risk, almost the entire team was searching the area.

It was my first search for a misper. It was winter, close to zero degrees, and I was frozen to the bone. Every late shift and night shift I wore about four layers but the cold and fatigue together meant I ended up shivering anyway. Jay, on the other hand, usually just wore the short-sleeved T-shirt. It was a bit of a competition within police stations (mostly between the men) to see who could bear wearing their short sleeves in cold temperatures.

During the search, Jay and I resumed our constant battle over the temperature of the car. It went like this: as soon as he was distracted or left the car, I would turn the heating up. As soon as he noticed it, he would turn it down. It went on like this for most of the shift until one of us gave up. Luckily, during the search, I found my police beanie in my pocket and I put it on.

The misper was eventually located. As soon as he spotted the officers – he ran.

I didn't know what to expect, but at Sully we'd been taught the importance of supporting vulnerable people. So when other officers ran the misper down and tackled him to the ground in the grass, I was a bit taken aback. I understood entirely that it was a reasonable use of force to protect the individual from harming themselves – after all, they were suicidal – but to see it in action was still a shock and felt counter-intuitive to me. A fresh reminder of how different the ICR policing was to how I had imagined it would be while training at Sully.

The search had taken hours. With it finished, we all returned to the station to warm up and complete paperwork. I kept my coat and beanie on for 15 minutes or so while sitting at my desk – I felt too cold to take them off. While I was working on the paperwork, a sergeant walked passed the desk and said:

"Someone needs to tell Jade how much I hate the beanies."

A ripple of disbelief spread over me as I tried to work out what to do with this passive aggressive remark. I couldn't get my head around it at all. Was that the most professionalism that a sergeant could manage? After I'd spent hours in the freezing cold doing good work, while he was sat in the warm office? On top of all the tiredness, the strangeness of the job, it felt like another punch in the gut. I decided to keep the beanie on for a little longer to warm up. After all, it was official police uniform, and if this sergeant didn't like it, he could come and talk to me about it like a grown up. My colleague laughed.

"Look at you, challenging authority. You're turning into Jay already."

CHAPTER 10

THE MOST THANKLESS PC JOBS

I still see the police recruitment ads sometimes. 'A career that matters' and 'help people' seem to be the main messages in those campaigns. They paint the picture that the role of police officer is one where you can help people and feel rewarded. And while this is undoubtedly true, the reality is slightly more nuanced. It's not all saving lives and solving crimes. There are many things they don't tell you in those ads about the daily work of a PC, including some truly thankless tasks. I did say this was about showing the entirety of my job as a police officer – so I'll mention a few here.

The first thankless task is called a 'cell watch'. It's for when you have a detainee who is a risk to themselves – possibly because they are trying to self-harm. Your job as a PC is to sit at their cell door with the door open, keeping your eyes inside the cell and on the detainee. Unsurprisingly, there's no phone scrolling or distractions of any kind. You're literally just staring at the detainee to make sure they don't come to any harm.

This can often go on for hours, if not a whole nine-hour shift – and I have done at least one cell watch that lasted the entire shift. If you're on a late or night shift, not falling asleep is quite challenging as you stare into their cell – usually watching them sleep.

The detainee I was watching had previously self-harmed and was known for 'dirty protests'. The sergeant on the team thought this would be a good opportunity for me to sign off 'conflict' from my portfolio in case the detainee lost his shit (literally). I sat by the cell door praying I would not get faeces thrown at me. Luckily, apart from a short rant about the housing crisis and a small meal break, the detainee spent most of the time asleep. That left me staring out into space for hours on end. Suddenly I realised what it reminded me of: detention when I was in high school. No distraction or entertainment, just sitting down and waiting for it to finish. As soon as that thought entered my head, I thought to myself 'that's not good. Have I chosen the right job here?'

I've also been on a 'bed watch'. This is where officers have to watch someone who's in hospital. This happens when a person is arrested and becomes ill while in custody or on the way to custody. Officers then escort the person to hospital and have to stand watch over them until they are ready to be discharged.

Bed watches happen quite often. Not because criminals are all in poor health, but because more seasoned criminals know that even if they feign illness and no one is really fooled, officers will still take them to hospital. The reason why criminals choose to do this has never been quite clear to me. As I mentioned before, it doesn't help run down the timer on how long they can be held – the PACE clock, as it's known, after the Police and Criminal Evidence Act 1984 that governs a lot of police powers, including how long you can hold someone without charge – so it just makes the whole process longer for everyone.

This whole issue brings us to one of the biggest unofficial jobs you have as a police officer: covering your own ass. Even if you are certain that someone's faking an illness, it's not worth the risk of refusing to take them to hospital. On the off-chance that they are indeed ill, you could face a lengthy misconduct procedure or even a criminal trial. So, no matter how badly someone fakes being ill in an attempt to delay being brought into police custody, their attempt will work.

A colleague on my team was involved in the arrest of a well-known burglar, and asked the suspect if he had anything on him he shouldn't have (a fairly standard question before searching someone). In an incredibly sarcastic tone, the suspect said:

"Yea, I've got drugs up my bum alright?!"

"Do you?" my colleague replied.

"No, of course I fucking haven't," the suspect replied. As it was such a flippant remark the officer decided to let it pass and brought him in. However, after a reflection with the rest of the team and our sergeant, the suspect was in fact taken to hospital. If he indeed had drugs up his bum and the packaging burst, he would have died. The officer should have brought the suspect to hospital regardless of whether he thought the suspect was lying or not. As the sergeant said: "don't risk losing your job over that idiot! Not worth it!"

My bed watch was for a high-risk domestic abuse suspect who we'll call Rahul. He'd been arrested at his ex-partner's address, and during the arrest he'd been tasered – but the taser hadn't connected, meaning that he hadn't actually received the shock. However, he was still complaining of heart palpitations due to the tasering when my colleague and I brought him in, so the custody sergeant did the right thing and sent him to hospital. At the time, I wondered why none of the ten officers involved in the actual arrest wanted to take him into custody. I soon found out.

In the A&E waiting room, I discovered that my suspect had a flair for theatrics.

"The police tasered me!" he loudly exclaimed to his captive audience, over and over again. "I was compliant and they still tasered me!"

Finally, we were shown into a separate room with a bed in it to wait to be seen. Rahul laid down and proceeded to spend the rest of my shift – a good eight hours – talking to us about the offence. I suspect he knew that we are not allowed to talk about the offence with the suspect. If we did, it would count as an official interview, which is against PACE procedures – and was doing it to rile us up. He kept telling us (as he had told everyone in the waiting room) that really he was being oppressed by police and that his ex-partner had an evil vendetta against him. He had, of course, failed to mention to the public in the waiting room that he was the one who broke into her house with a knife.

I've never wished physical violence on anyone, but Rahul came very close to pushing me over the edge. At the end of my shift, he was still there waiting to be seen – not surprising, since the initial triage had probably ascertained that he was absolutely fine. From that moment on, I appreciated the offenders who just had the decency to stay silent a lot more.

The next painful task you can get allocated as a PC is a 'scene watch'. This is where a crime scene needs to be guarded to make sure no one enters without permission and compromises the integrity of the crime scene. Just as with the others, a scene watch can be hours at a time, even a whole shift. You might think that it sounds quite relaxing – with all the pressure and intensity of the rest of the work, a shift spent watching a quiet scene is a welcome break, right? I never had to do a scene watch myself, but I spoke to plenty of people who did – and they disagreed. In the first place, you aren't always going to be sat on a park bench in the sunshine, watching over a scene. You might be standing in the freezing cold in the dead of night watching over an abandoned house, stood in a thunderstorm in a field – anything. Secondly, the monotony is just as bad as it is with a cell watch.

A case in point – though a slightly strange example – was when the automatic gate into the police station's car park broke so that it remained open and wouldn't shut (a frequent occurrence as the gate was temperamental). Until the engineers arrived to fix it, the open gate presented a security risk. Any member of the public could now gain access to the police yard. So, a PC would need to guard the gate to ensure that only authorised people got in – essentially, a scene watch. I remember arriving early one morning to find a not-so-fresh faced PC guarding the broken gate. We spoke and I found out that he'd been there since the evening before – an entire shift spent guarding a broken gate. Not really the heroic or action-packed job many envisage when they think of the police.

Lastly, and unfortunately, there was the 'poo watch'. If a detainee is suspected of having swallowed drugs to conceal them (rather than taking them), officers have to sit and wait by their cell until they empty their bowels. This is for the welfare of the detainee – it's not unheard of for the packaging to burst – and potentially to gather evidence of an offence.

I count myself very lucky that I was never on a poo watch, but the stories from others who have done it painted a pretty grim picture. As soon as the person empties their bowels, you have to be nearby to sift through the contents to check for the drugs (the toilets in cells are specifically designed so that you can inspect someone's poo or wee if you need to). Part of the reason why you have to be very near when they go to the toilet is the risk of the detainee re-swallowing the drugs after they've just pooed them out.

There's an article you can read on Sky news about a detainee who was on a poo watch for 47 days without emptying his bowels. It was the longest stand-off I've ever read about. I don't even know how that's possible. Finally, the police were "forced to release the suspect on medical and legal advice", though he was later rearrested for a different offence.

Finally - a term I became familiar with early on during my work in ICR was the 'Slough job'. This was a term used to refer to an outrageous and often shitty case. It often involved the victim being a well-known criminal who was not planning to give any statements, answer any calls, or cooperate with the police in any way. Sometimes a third party had seen what was going on and called the police, other times the criminal themselves had called to ensure their immediate safety – but however it happened, it always ended with the victim ghosting the police.

I mention these jobs so that the next time you see a shiny recruitment ad for the police which states that you can 'make a difference' and 'protect the vulnerable', you'll know that if you are tempted to join up, you will probably also end up on a cell watch, bed watch or worst case, poo watch alongside all the other jobs they do tell you about.

I honestly wish that they told these kinds of stories more often at recruitment events. Not to try and scare people off – I don't think it would have changed my mind about my decision to go into the police – but because people deserve to know about the job in its entirety. Certainly, the people that remain interested after hearing about the poo watch are the people you want to hire.

CHAPTER 11

DOMESTICS, ADULT PROTECTION, AND SLEEP

It's the end of a long evening shift. 22:00. It's been quiet for a while and I'm driving back to the station with Jay to hand over to the nightshift team. A voice on the radio breaks the silence.

"Anyone free for a grade 1 domestic?"

Silence.

Grade 1 is the most urgent kind of job, going down to grade 4. ICR generally only attended grade 1 and 2 jobs, while grades 3 and 4 are often dealt with by appointment, entirely over the phone, or online.

I look at Jay. He shakes his head.

We wait but no one responds.

"If no one volunteers I'm going to allocate it to someone," the voice of the sergeant crackles over the radio. Still no one replies, and so car ZC35 is allocated the job – not us. We head back to the station as planned.

'Domestics' as they are called are the most hated jobs by response officers. Not because they don't care about domestic abuse, but because most domestic jobs aren't actually about violent or abusive relationships. Most of them are petty arguments where someone has called the police to intervene – either a well-intentioned neighbour, or one of the people arguing in a bid to win the argument. But because domestic abuse is such a huge risk for the victim and so prevalent in communities, it's a huge priority for TVP and you absolutely cannot get it wrong. So every time you go to a domestic, you have to follow all the steps to the letter. It's just not worth the risk of not taking any action with something that looks like a little spat about nothing, only to find later that it's part of a larger pattern of abuse that leaves a victim hurt or killed. And while I totally agree with that, breaking up all those little spats is both frustrating and a drain on your time – both on patrol and back at the station doing paperwork.

Not too long ago, Jay and I had rushed on blue lights to a domestic incident which turned out to be a mother and son having an argument over vegan food. The son (a 17-year-old know-it-all) didn't want to eat animal products for religious reasons – yet the mother had made him a meal with fish in it. The mother called the police to try and scare her son, hoping that the officers would put him in his place. Jay was furious.

"I can't believe I drove here on blue lights, risking the life of myself and my colleague, to teach you how to parent and you how to show respect to your parents!" He'd shouted.

Domestics which turn out to be petty arguments rather than a crime are referred to as a 'dom-non'. Even so, officers have to proceed with a Dash risk assessment (also called a DOM5 in TVP) with the victim. Dash stands for "domestic abuse, stalking and honour-based abuse", and is aimed at helping police, other emergency responders and frontline practitioners identify the risk level present. It's a good tool, and an important one, but it's also a long and arduous questionnaire, with questions such as "has (s)he ever tried to drown, suffocate, or choke you?" and "Does (s)he do things of a sexual nature that make you feel bad?" The score of the assessment will roughly indicate whether the relationship is high, medium or standard risk.

Police are supposed to complete a Dash risk assessment at every incident labelled as domestic abuse – even if you visit the same address, for the same people, a hundred times. Every time, you're supposed to do the assessment – and because domestics are so high-risk for everyone involved, we never skipped one, no matter how tedious it felt. When it comes to dom-non cases, you have the added hassle of deciding who is the victim. If there's no crime, how can there be a victim? We'll touch on this more later, but it can be quite the headache when you're filling in a Dash risk assessment.

Some weeks later, Jay and I were on a nightshift and received a call from the control room while out patrolling. A man had called in an extremely agitated state telling the operator he had chased a group of youths down the road who had tried to break into his house. The man had apparently sworn a lot and expressed his displeasure with the police. As we set off, I could see Jay was already getting slightly annoyed with this man and was preparing to give him a telling off.

We found the man in the middle of an empty street (it was 3am). Jay rolled down the window as the man approached.

"You're too late now!" he snapped. "Why weren't you here 10 minutes ago?!" and with that he started walking back to his house.

Jay bit his tongue for a moment and told the man we'd meet him back at his house, a few hundred metres down the road. I got out of the car and walked up to the front door, where the man was standing in the doorway.

"What happened?" I asked him.

He made another reference to us being too late and I acknowledged that it would have been better if we were here earlier – he wasn't wrong, even if we'd got there as fast as we could. Thankfully, the man seemed to have calmed down a lot.

"OK, then," he said, "do you want to know? Come in." and he gestured us into his house.

"Do you want to take a seat?" he asked. We both politely declined, which is relatively common in these situations. It's sometimes a matter of hygiene (though this guy's house wasn't too messy or dirty), and sometimes a matter of not wanting to give the impression you're going to stay for a long time.

With that, the man leapt into a monologue which was very hard to follow. The youths that he'd supposedly chased down after they'd broken into his house didn't feature in the story at all. Instead, he told us about his son and the fact that he was a one percenter with the Hell's Angels or a similar motorbike club. Jay and I both listened without saying a word for about ten minutes, other than to add the occasional nod or 'mmm hmm' sound.

The story was very chaotic and incoherent. The man jumped from emotion to emotion without much context – one moment he was angry, the next boastful – and then he started crying. I asked him whether there was anything we could do for him, but he didn't give me a clear answer. Instead, he started talking again about the motorbike club and his son. After another five minutes had passed, Jay and I made eye contact. He made a small facial expression to me and pointed to the door with his eyes. We both had to hide a smile at the absurdity of the situation. It took a few attempts to end the conversation but about 20 minutes later we walked out to our car again.

It was clear to both of us that this was a mental health-related incident and that there were no burglars. Honestly, the story was so incoherent that I wasn't even entirely sure that the man even had a son (I checked this on the system later but couldn't find any confirmation either way). Jay turned to me in the car and said,

"Please don't tell me you believed his story about him being in the Hells Angels..."

I laughed and shook my head.

When we got back to the station, we completed an adult protection form for the man. This is a form which is shared with the MASH (multi-agency safeguarding hub) which allows us to share safeguarding concerns with relevant agencies. Although the call hadn't resulted in us catching any criminals, I was pleased that we'd gone and listened to the man – even if he had started out quite cross with us. It was good to flag him to other agencies to make sure he was looked after, and I definitely got the sense that he had nobody to talk to in his life – so to have two of us listen to him hopefully made a difference.

My period in uniform was by far the most exhausting of my life. As the weeks wore on, though, I found myself struggling more and more to cope with the exhaustion of the job. I mentioned before that you work six days in a row – two earlies, two lates, two nights, and then four days off. In practice, though, the first day is spent sleeping, so you only had three days to actually do anything. And because I was on the DC DHEP course, my time off was often spent working on assignments for my course. Before starting, I'd always assumed the shift pattern would be more stable: a few weeks on night shifts, then evening shifts, then earlies. However, doing all three shift patterns in one working week ensures that your natural rhythm is completely disrupted.

I slept very poorly and got hungry at the strangest moments. And every time, as we got to the end of the six days my exhaustion level reached absurd levels. At work, my brain felt like mush. I could barely remember my own name, let alone take in all the detail needed to handle the various types of jobs we went out to. Every time we were allocated a job by control, they relayed the information – circumstances, address, and so on – verbally. I just couldn't hold on to that information when I was tired. I had to ask for it again and again until I could either write it down or it would finally stick in my brain.

Of course, I asked my colleagues how they dealt with the crushing routine. The only advice I ever got to try and cope was to get two hours of sleep before coming to work. I tried it, but I couldn't make it work. I've always had a very rigid body clock; sleeping on command has never worked for me. On top of that, the pressure of this particular situation made sleep impossible. I'd lie down to sleep before a shift, and my brain would start to dwell on the importance of the sleep. 'You HAVE to sleep now!' it would shout. 'If you don't, the next eight hours will be hell!' Unsurprisingly, I never managed to get that sleep.

Jay would sometimes doze off towards the end of the night shifts while we were back in the office. He would sit at his desk scrolling through TikTok videos and slowly nod off. During the nap his finger would often continue scrolling.

After the night shifts, I struggled to drive home. At the start of every commute home, I had a little adrenaline left over from my shift, but within 15 minutes of driving that would fade and I would be overcome by the most incredible urge to sleep. I'd never worried before about falling asleep behind the wheel; I don't usually get tired behind the wheel, and certainly not to the stage where I'm nodding off. This level of exhaustion was different though. I didn't exactly fall asleep at the wheel; it was more like miniature blackouts, which I later discovered are referred to medically as microsleeps. One second, my eyes would be as wide open as I could force them, looking at the road; the next thing I knew my head was down, looking at the pedals. A microsleep can last up to 15 seconds, and is a common symptom of exhaustion. Your brain doesn't completely shut down like when you go to sleep normally, but your responsiveness to external stimuli is reduced, and often you're not even aware that you're microsleeping. It was completely involuntary, and it was pretty scary – shift workers are three times as likely to experience a car crash as non-shift workers, and I imagine microsleeps are quite likely a big cause of that.

I experienced these microsleeps a few times while driving home from work. To fight them I opened the windows, hoping that the noise and wind would stop my body and brain from shutting down. When this wasn't enough, I put the radio on and sang at the top of my lungs. Surely, I reasoned, you can't fall asleep while singing at full volume? That worked reasonably well but I had to sing constantly. If I stopped for even a fraction of a second, I would find myself nodding again.

I considered stopping on the hard shoulder a few times, but sleeping on the hard shoulder didn't seem particularly safe either – and in any case, a fairly long stretch of the road home didn't have a hard shoulder so I wouldn't have been able to pull over even if I wanted to.

It was only after I finished my ten weeks in uniform and my shift pattern changed to a more consistent one that I realised how dangerous my driving was during this time. I could have killed someone – or myself. I decided afterwards to never drive in that state again – and I was lucky that my time in the police was never that physically exhausting again.

Of course, thinking back now I can't have been the only one driving around in this state – we were all working through the same conditions, after all. And sadly, I don't see an obvious alternative to it. Because a shift could (and regularly did) go into overtime depending on what you were doing, getting home by public transport wasn't reliable – if you finished after the busses or trains had finished you'd be stranded. Most of the officers came to work by car for this reason. And there was nowhere to sleep at the station, even if you'd wanted to. From my perspective, changing the shift patterns so that you were on the same shift for a longer period of time would help because your body would adjust to each shift pattern and you'd be less tired. But there were also officers who preferred the rotating shift pattern to a fixed one – so perhaps I was in the minority.

I still regret driving while that tired. I was very lucky not to have crashed and hurt someone else or myself. Unfortunately, many officers before me have. There's a charity called Care of Police Survivors (or COPS for short) who compile a video every year memorialising officers who died in the line of duty that year. Several died in car crashes on their way home from work after long shifts. It was very surreal to look at those faces and realise that they could have been me.

CHAPTER 12

WEXHAM PARK ASSAULT

The weeks in ICR ground on, a blur of exhaustion, adrenaline, and (still) feeling out of my depth. I started feeling nauseous all the time. Then I experienced two to three days of vomiting, and five days of extreme nausea. I was unable to eat, unable to stand up, which after five days culminated in a panic attack and a trip to A&E. I was off work for about a week. The tests at hospital had not found anything.

"It's probably the stress," my dad told me. He'd come over to help me after I'd returned home from A&E.

The thought of that unsettled me. I'd been stressed before, of course, but the most that had ever affected me physically was to give me a stiff neck or back pain. I really wanted a diagnosis of some (temporary) illness; I hated the idea of being so ill because of something so intangible. Plus, what was I supposed to do about it? I couldn't see any way to make my job less stressful. Thankfully, the time off work enabled me to recover enough to carry on – though my ten weeks in uniform had been extended slightly because of it, and I hated the idea of being paid to sit around doing nothing.

"Are you OK?" Jay said when I finally got back. "I thought I was going to have to send flowers to your family for the funeral."

I liked Jay. He knew when some light-hearted humour was the right thing, and when to be serious.

So, despite the extension to my time in ICR, the end was finally in sight. I got back into the rhythm (such as it was) of the job. It was at this point that

I started to have my first twinges of disappointment with the justice system that we were a part of.

It was a Saturday night, around 10pm, and I was on a late shift until 3am – on Fridays and Saturdays the late shift was extended since we were busier. I was crewed with another officer this time (Jay was on another deployment) and I just had that 'shit is going to hit the fan tonight' feeling.

Soon we were called to Wexham Park hospital – sadly a place we were often called to. Control room relayed a message that a man had become violent in A&E and attacked nurses and an ambulance worker – and had bitten part of the ambulance worker's arm off. I was shocked and taken aback by the report. Someone had part of their arm bitten off?! This guy must be way out of control, I thought to myself.

When we arrived at the hospital we ran through the corridors, trying to find the incident. Finding the right department at Wexham park always felt like solving a maze to me; luckily, this time staff were pointing us in the right direction. When we arrived at the right department, I saw the guy was already in handcuffs and being held down by four hospital security guards and one police officer. Another officer had beaten us to the location and handcuffed the suspect.

The suspect was a tall skinny man. My colleague and I had arrived in a van, so once the suspect was ready to be taken outside the four security guards escorted him back to our van, with me at the lead to open the van doors. Just before the suspect was put inside the van, he started resisting again. He started kicking the guards and hurling abuse as they tried to keep him under control.

"FUCKING PAKI!" he shouted to one of the guards.

With this, the suspect was taken to the ground by the guards, and my colleague and I joined in to put leg restraints on him. At the same time, I arrested him for a racially aggravated public order offence.

As soon as we put him in the back of the van he started spitting so my colleague put a spit hood on him, and I further arrested him for criminal damage on the police van. Temporary damage to police property – like spitting on a van – counts as criminal damage. For example, in *R v Fiak [2005] EWCA Crim 2381* the defendant flooded his cell by pushing a blanket down the toilet and flushing repeatedly. This was considered criminal damage because the cell and blanket were not usable for a period of time.

Anyway, back to the van, with the suspect wearing his spit hood in the cage. We left him there to cool his heels while I spoke to my crew mate about the details of the incident such as victims and witnesses. Before I updated the control room he told me that the suspect had not, in fact, bitten a part of the victim's arm off. He had bitten him on the side of his torso, hard enough to leave a bite mark. The suspect had also racially abused other NHS staff members. I was perplexed as to how that false piece of information about the victim having part of his arm bitten off made it into the crime report. Looking back with more experience, it was not unusual for there to be wrong information in the crime report. That's why as an officer, you can't ever take the initial report at face value – you have to check and double check all the facts again when you arrive at the scene. If nothing else, sometimes other things have happened since the initial report that are important and need to be recorded, too. I never got to the bottom of why it was so common for information on the report to be wrong. I suspect that a lot of the time it was because the person making the report – usually a member of the public – was in a state of distress or upset at the time and so got some of the details wrong.

Unfortunately, the suspect in the cage of the van did not lower his aggression levels so a colleague and I (both of us probationary officers) had to restrain him in the back of the van while my crew mate drove us to the station. The suspect focused his verbal abuse on me now. I am not sure why he targeted me specifically, but I believe it might have been because I was the only female officer there.

"YOU UGLY SLAG!"

"NO MAN WILL EVER TOUCH YOU!"

"YOU FILTHY WHORE!"

The abuse was vile, and it carried on for the entire 40-minute drive to the station.

"I WILL RAPE YOU."

"I WILL RAPE YOUR ENTIRE FAMILY."

"I WILL STAB YOU, YOU SLAG!"

At this stage my crew mate shouted at me from the front of the van that I should arrest him for the offence of 'Fear or provocation of violence' under section 4 of the public order act. I felt instinctively that this was pointless, but I took the advice of a much more experienced colleague and further arrested the suspect. It didn't stop the abuse.

There was another moment during the drive where the suspect turned to the other probationer with whom I was restraining the suspect, a young man, and said:

"Get your hands off me, you gay boy."

At the time I was busy blocking out the torrent of abuse so didn't really register it, but I later found out that he was further arrested for this phrase in interview as this counted as a hate crime. In fact, we were criticised for not arresting the suspect for this at the time it happened. My crew mate, the driver, was quick to throw me under the bus.

"I told you to do it! Why didn't you?" he said. I thought about calling him out on the fact that he most definitely had not told me to do it, or asking him why he didn't make the arrest himself once we got there, but by that point in the shift I simply couldn't be bothered with any more aggravation.

Later, in line with my instincts, CPS refused to charge him with the crime of fear or provocation of violence against me. They quoted a piece of caselaw which essentially explains that officers should have thicker skin than the average member of the public. As an officer, you have to accept it when someone threatens to rape you, stab you and rape your family. He was charged for the 'gay boy' comment, however – officers are not expected to put up with discriminatory language.

Looking back, that decision is at once absolutely shocking to me, and also not at all surprising. Threats of sexual violence made towards female officers are their own form of discrimination. After all, the suspect didn't threaten to rape anyone else in the van. And violence against women and girls was also a very high priority for TVP and other police forces across the country. But as I say, on one level it's not surprising. The CPS won't charge a case if there's no realistic prospect of conviction. But it's astonishing that with such a priority at the time being placed on violence against women and girls, that they thought there was a low chance of conviction.

The offences committed by the suspect became my first investigation to manage as OIC (officer in the case), which means you have responsibility for the case and the investigation. And by God, I was determined to get this one through. I felt incredibly strongly about it. Not just because of my own experiences with the suspect – thankfully, his threats and insults didn't stick with me after the event – but because of the impact it had had on the NHS workers at Wexham Park. They were left afraid to come into work, scared that something similar might happen again – or that he might come back to terrorise them again. To indulge in a cliché for a moment, I really wanted to nail the bastard.

CHAPTER 13

LAST WEEK ON ICR

After an overwhelming and relentless period on response, it was my last week with ICR. Unfortunately for me, that feeling of drowning had never really gone away during my time in ICR. I had hoped it would get better as I got more competent and adapted to the schedule, but although the learning curve was steep, there was still so much more to learn. I hear that some people learn under pressure. I am probably the opposite. I learned well at the training centre, when there was little pressure and the consequences of my mistakes were minimal. But the yawning chasm between the job our training had prepared us for and the realities of life in uniform had put me (and other rookies) at a severe disadvantage. Between unlearning things we'd been taught at Sully, the mountain of new things to learn, the stress, and the sleep deprivation, taking in new information seemed impossible.

I continued to struggle to memorise things. Information would come from the control room thick and fast when you were out on patrol: we might be told to be on the lookout for a white BMW, registration Hotel Mike 53, Lima Papa Mike, being driven by an IC1 male (IC codes indicate ethnicity – IC 1 is 'white – North European') wearing dark jeans, green T-shirt, black puffer jacket, brown short hair, black cap, white shoes with a stripe.

Under normal circumstances I would be able to keep this information in my short-term memory and retain it long enough to copy it down. However, during the late shifts and night shifts when I was fighting the urge to sleep, no information stuck. Luckily Jay remembered everything perfectly, which gave me hope that with experience I could too. Other officers did tell me that it got easier with time, too. But at this point in my career, if Jay hadn't been there, I'd probably have had to call back to the control room about four times to confirm a house number or a street name. Generally, the information was being relayed so quickly that I didn't have time to take out my notebook and pen to get it all down. I often hoped desperately that the next name or street address would be something plain and easy to spell. John Smith, living on Green Street, or something. It usually wasn't.

For a while, I kept my pocket notebook in the central holder of the car so I could quickly grab it to make notes. However, that resulted in me forgetting it in the car when we finished our shift, which led to a small telling off.

Despite these challenges, I continued doing my best. One story I remember from this period was when Jay and I were assigned to another high-risk misper search. This time it was a 13-year-old boy with autism who had run away from the hospital and was missing. We drove to the hospital to speak to the mother, who was the one who had reported her son missing.

"I saw it coming," she said, sick with worry. "The hospital staff weren't listening to me." She sighed. "I knew my son was getting overwhelmed in the hospital waiting room. There were too many people, too many sounds. He cannot handle that."

Jay and I asked some further questions to see where he could have gone and joined the search with other officers already searching. We were driving around the main roads leading away from the hospital with a digital picture of the boy on our phones.

"Are you feeling sprightly today?" Jay said with a smile.

"Why? What do you mean?" I replied.

"Well, just saying. If we find him. He's going to run."

That struck me as weird, but it's more common than you'd think. I'm certainly not an expert on autism and other mental health conditions, but if the boy had been overwhelmed by all the noise and people around him to the point of having to flee, it makes sense that he'd do anything to avoid going back – including running from the police. Plus, of course, a large group of unfamiliar police officers coming after you is, in its own way, just as overwhelming as a waiting room full of noisy people.

In the end, another crew located the boy and brought him back to his mother who was waiting for him. When I arrived back at the hospital, I saw a shy looking boy sitting in the police van next to his mum his face covered in tears. After someone's been missing the police fill in a(nother) form with some information about the missing episode, including basic things like where they went, why they went missing, and whether they need any support. After we finished the report we walked back to our car, and I looked back and smiled at the boy. I'll never forget how he looked as he meekly waved goodbye to me, face still wet with tears. So often in the police I found myself dealing with challenging people – those who didn't want to be helped, those who were violent, those who were setting out to break the law. And then here was this sweet little boy. It was plain to see that he didn't have a bad bone in his body. He wasn't looking for trouble. He was just struggling to cope with the world around him. He reminded me a little of the misper we looked for in the freezing cold who ran and was taken down. Although they were both different people, suffering with very different conditions, they were both being driven to extreme courses of action because of their mental health. It wasn't their fault. Though it felt good to help him, it was also hard to watch such a sweet kid struggling like that. I can still see him now in my memory, clear as day.

In that last week I also went to enforce a closure order on a trap house – that's a house that's used in the drug trade. Also known as drug dens, crack houses, or shooting galleries, trap houses are places where criminals can sell drugs, and users can take them.

A closure order is a court order that prohibits access to a property for a specific period of time. To directly quote the legislation:

The çourt may make a closure order if it is satisfied—

a) that a person has engaged, or (if the order is not made) is likely to engage, in disorderly, offensive or criminal behaviour on the premises, or

b) that the use of the premises has resulted, or (if the order is not made) is likely to result, in serious nuisance to members of the public, or

c) that there has been, or (if the order is not made) is likely to be, disorder near those premises associated with the use of those premises, and that the order is necessary to prevent the behaviour, nuisance or disorder from continuing, recurring or occurring.

This closure order was for the property, rather than individuals or specific circumstances – meaning that nobody was allowed in, full stop, while the closure order was in force. I went to enforce the order with the neighbourhood policing team. Which is a good time to quickly explain the difference between ICR and Neighbourhood policing.

Both ICR and Neighbourhood police officers can be found out on the streets – but Neighbourhood police teams don't generally respond to emergency calls. Their role is to be much more closely embedded in the community, forming close links with people and helping keep communities safe. In that way, they're much closer to the round-faced, slightly bumbling police officers you see in Poirot or Downton Abbey, than ICR. They're the teams who intervene in neighbourhood disputes and enforce closure orders in their communities.

When we got into the trap house, using keys provided by the landlord, it was disgusting beyond my wildest dreams. You couldn't see the floor for all the rubbish covering it. Mattresses lay on the floor in various locations, riddled with lice. The toilet was an abomination. And, of course, since this was a trap house, needles were on every surface. It was such a health hazard that the CSI teams weren't actually allowed in to gather evidence.

One of our jobs was to see if there was anyone in the house – and if so, remove them. Thankfully, there was nobody in at the time. Once that was established, we sealed up the house – though my exhaustion was such that looking back now, I honestly have no idea what exactly we did to effectively seal it. It shocked me that people would actually spend time in a house that awful – including sleeping there and using the bathroom.

There was also a 'concern for welfare' job that stood out to me at this time. I was on my last set of late shifts, on patrol with several colleagues in a police van. We received a grade 1 call. It was a concern for welfare; a support worker had reported concerns about a man she worked with, and was concerned he may have taken an overdose. The van sped off on blue lights, siren blaring.

I was at that upper limit of exhaustion that got me every time I was on late shifts or night shifts. Normally, this meant that my head was bobbing constantly; every time it did, I woke with a gasp and looked around, embarrassed. I didn't want to sleep at work. I wanted to be lucid and sharp, ready to deal with whatever incident presented itself to me. But I just couldn't deny my body's need for sleep.

I slept for most of the journey despite the blue lights and sirens. When I got out of the van, adrenaline kicked in – combined with the few minutes of sleep, that gave me a slight bump of energy and lucidity.

My colleague Sam went into the property first. I followed behind her. The property was a hostel – lots of rooms housing people, sometimes in dorm-style bunk rooms. The hostel manager told us the room number where we could find the man, who we'll call Aaron. We went up the stairs and my colleague knocked.

"Aaron! It's the police."

Aaron swung open the door. His brow furrowed and his chest pumped forward.

"What the fuck do you want?" he demanded. Not a great start.

"We came to see if you're OK," my colleague replied.

"I'm fine. Now fuck off!" Aaron retorted, raising his voice.

"Your support worker is concerned you took an overdose," she replied.

"I told you, I'm fucking fine!" Aaron shouted.

"How about you come outside and we can talk properly?" My colleague asked.

Aaron stepped out of sight behind the door and returned to the door in a bladed stance – one foot in front of the other, with the body at an angle. He also had one hand behind his back, which made me nervous.

"What have you got behind your back?" I said to him.

"Nothing," he replied, showing us the hand behind his back. It was empty, and I wasn't sure if he was carrying something or not, but the situation was clearly escalating and I was not sure how to proceed. He said he was fine, and currently seemed fine, although he was very hostile and aggressive. Were we supposed to take him at his word? He had a support worker so was clearly vulnerable in some sense. Did we have power to enter and check whether he was OK?

I might have been unsure about how to proceed, but a male officer who was with us was not. He simply walked into the room and started to look around. His reaction told us at least that Aaron was unarmed – but his actions very obviously infuriated Aaron. He started to get very close in the officer's face, telling him fuck off.

"Can we go hands-on, please," said my sergeant who was standing in the hallway. The way she said it was so languid; she had a posh accent, although it always sounded artificial to me.

Aaron, meanwhile, exploded with rage.

"YOU WANT TO GO HANDS-ON WITH ME?! I WILL FUCK YOU UP!"

At that, all officers present jumped on him and one sprayed him with PAVA spray. In short order he was restrained on the bed in his room and placed in handcuffs. All the while, he was shouting a barrage of abuse towards us:

"CUNTS! PIGS!"

The abuse continued as we escorted him down the stairs and into the police van, his eyes red and streaming with tears, snot coming out of his nose.

Since the initial call had been about concerns of an overdose, we took Aaron to hospital. While in the van he started fixating on a few officers. Staring intensely at them. Telling them he would find out where they lived and come find them. He continued his barrage of verbal abuse until we arrived at the hospital. By that time everyone had given up trying to talk to him or calm him down. Thankfully, unlike the Wexham Park incident I was largely left alone by this suspect. And since you're no doubt wondering, nobody arrested Aaron for fear or provocation of violence. I guess it just didn't occur to anyone – me included.

When we arrived at the hospital, only two officers stayed behind and the rest, including me, went back on patrol. The last I saw of Aaron, he was being placed into a wheelchair and rolled inside the hospital. After I got back to the station, I approached a colleague who was there at the address.

"So, what power did we use to drag that guy out of his house like that?" I asked.

"Mental Capacity Act," he replied.

Even though I did not have extensive knowledge of the Mental Capacity Act, I knew that couldn't be true. There was nothing to suggest Aaron did not have capacity to make his own decisions.

I felt very uneasy about the whole incident. The reality was that, on the one hand, if the police had taken Aaron's word for it and left, and he did overdose and die, we would have failed in our duty to protect him and his death would have been our fault. On the other hand, we PAVA sprayed someone and dragged him out of his house, just so we could cover ourselves. I don't know whether we did have the powers to enter his room and forcibly take him to hospital. The only thing that gave me a sense of comfort was that the sergeant was there and had given the orders. There were also other officers with many years of experience. I guess they knew the right course of action to take? Still, it didn't feel right at all.

The next day I saw one of my colleagues who had stayed with Aaron in hospital.

"What happened at hospital?" I asked.

"He calmed down, actually" the officer replied. I was quite surprised to hear it given the level of anger he had shown all the way to the hospital, though relieved that he hadn't been more difficult. He hadn't taken an overdose so after a check-up he was able to go back home.

One of the very last things I did during my time in ICR, and one of the last things I needed to tick off my portfolio, was interviewing. I asked my sergeant whether I could observe an interview first before leading one – by now I knew that everything we learnt at training school was wildly different in the real world, so I wanted to try and find out what was different before I had to interview someone for real. Unfortunately, when it came to it, there was no time.

We had a couple in custody for a domestic incident which had happened the previous night. The girl had a broken finger and the guy a bruise on his eyebrow. I was instructed to interview the girl – so frantic preparation began. You never get much time to prep for interviews. You receive pressure from the custody team as soon as you get allocated the task.

"Are you on your way?"

"The solicitor is waiting…"

"The PACE clock is running out."

PACE is the main piece of legislation covering a large part of police powers and procedures, and it dictates how long we can hold a suspect without charging them. In that time we need to conduct any interviews we need to, and gather all evidence we can to try and get a charge.

Despite time pressure I had prepared a structured and detailed interview plan. It even had prompts in case I forgot any of the mandatory information to give at the start of the interview. That information includes the time and date, the interview room number, police station where the interview is taking place, people present in the room, the caution and you have to remind the suspect of their right to legal advice amongst other things.

I set off to the custody suite with another, more experienced officer from my team who would be second interviewer. I felt nervous but satisfied with my interview plan and the prep I had done. I walked up to the custody desk to speak to the custody sergeant to tell him we were here to interview cell five.

Custody sergeants are notorious for their grumpiness. In their defence, they are under a lot of pressure. The welfare of detainees is their responsibility; if a detainee dies in custody, the custody sergeant will be investigated and scrutinised. And deaths in custody are a very real possibility. A vast range of people are taken into custody every day: people with complex needs, drug users or dealers smuggling drugs into custody in their bodily orifices, people with serious mental health issues. So while nobody really enjoys dealing with a custody sergeant, we always tried not to take it personally – it was just the job.

The custody sergeant ignored me for some time while he continued typing – not unusual treatment from a custody sergeant. Suddenly, we were approached by a colleague that I'd been crewed with that day.

"Change of plan," they said. "You need to interview the guy instead."

"What?" I stammer, panic blossoming inside me. "I can't! I haven't prepared at all for that."

"You'll be fine," came the usual response. It turned out that another officer was already interviewing the woman, so I had no choice but to interview the man – the PACE clock was ticking, and I didn't have the time to go and redo all my preparation. I knew I had to improvise as I went.

The guy had not requested a solicitor, so I took him straight to the interview room from his cell. He seemed friendly and strangely comfortable.

I sat down in the interview room. All the Thames Valley Police interview rooms were small, colourless rooms with no windows. The chairs and table are made extra heavy so that they cannot be picked up and thrown. They are so heavy that even moving them an inch is a bit of a struggle. On the interviewer's side of the table there's a red strip on the wall which is a panic alarm. If you get attacked during interview you can press the strip and other officers in custody will come to support you. There are cameras in each corner of the room visually recording the interview. It's not a welcoming environment.

I struggle to put the blank interview disc into the recorder and start the recorder (we never used one at the training centre). My colleague helps me. 'Great,' I think, 'now I look like a newbie right from the start.' Once the discs are loaded and the machine set up properly I hit the record button.

"Today is the third of March, the time is eleven past three, we are in interview room 1 in Maidenhead Police station. My name is Jade Cameron." I also give my shoulder number, and ask the suspect to state his name and date of birth for the tape. He does. After having gone through the required information I start with the first question. We are trained to start with open questions.

"You were arrested for assault yesterday. Can you tell me exactly what happened?"

To my surprise, the suspect begins to talk.

"Shall I just tell you everything from the start?"

"Yes." I try and contain my surprise.

He starts talking about the day before the arrest, what he and his girlfriend did, what they talked about, an argument they had, their relationship in general. I am putting everything into concentrating on what he's saying. I want to make sure I write notes and take in everything that's said, while also thinking of follow up questions.

The suspect gives a lot of information but little of it is relevant to the assault. I don't want to interrupt this free flow of information, though. When we get to the assault he laughs at the absurdity of it.

"I never thought it would get to this. Both of us in a police cell. Right, so she thought I was cheating coz she saw a text from another girl on my phone. We started arguing about it and she started punching me." He pointed to the bruise on his eyebrow. "As more punches were flying in, I grabbed both her hands to stop her from punching me."

It transpires that, a little later, the girlfriend shouted at him that he'd broken her finger, and showed him the top half of her finger which was pointing at a slight angle. I continue asking more questions to get further detail.

"Where were you?"

"What was said between you?"

The interview lasted over an hour and when I finally hit the stop button on the tape I felt mentally exhausted. I escorted the suspect back to his cell and told him we'd tell him asap what would happen next.

The woman had given a 'no comment' interview, and during the interview with the guy I had a strong intuitive feeling he was telling the truth: that she had thrown the first punch and that he simply defended himself. I believed what he said, and so did my colleague. However, you absolutely can't rely on that feeling when investigating a case – the human brain is too full of unconscious biases and preconceptions. It was one of those domestic cases where it wasn't clear who the victim was.

The guy was released with bail conditions not to contact his girlfriend.

"Is it OK though if I help her book her train home?" he asked.

"No," we said.

Incidentally, we ended up driving the man home. I would have never imagined before joining the police that after interviewing and releasing someone from custody you would sometimes give them a ride. Obviously, it's done at the officer's discretion and you would normally only consider doing it if the person does not pose a risk to you.

I felt the interview had gone OK, and I was keen to hear my colleague's feedback.

"Really good for a first interview, mate!" he said.

I was chuffed. Despite all the hardship it confirmed to me I had done the right thing joining the detective fast track programme.

The challenges of my time in ICR had put a serious dent in my confidence; it had been harder than anything I was expecting, and didn't get easier as time went by. The stress had affected my physical health. On top of that – and perhaps I was being naïve here – my new colleagues had seemed much more cynical than I was expecting. I remember summing up in my head that whenever a job came in, the attitude was less 'hey, let's do a great job!' and more 'oh no, how do we get rid of this job?' All of this had planted the seed of doubt that perhaps I'd chosen the wrong career. Quite a come down from my time at Sully, where I'd been convinced this was the last job I'd ever have. And, speaking of Sully, the shock of discovering how far removed our training was from the realities of policing had been very difficult to take. I'd been banking on my training to prepare me for the job I'd chosen, and I'd been let down spectacularly in that regard.

So, to hear that I'd done my interview well was a real boost, and renewed my confidence in my career choice. Perhaps it was just that I wasn't cut out for life on response – which was fine, because that wasn't the job I'd signed up to do anyway. Skills like interviewing were much more in line with what my life as an investigator would be like.

When I left my final ICR shift, it felt like a weight had been lifted from my shoulders. Next up was the Priority Crime Team, and I was looking forward to finally starting my detective work and getting a chance to put different skills to the test.

PART 3

PRIORITY CRIME TEAM

CHAPTER 14

WELCOME TO PCT

PCT, or the Priority Crime Team, lived upstairs in Slough police station. Unlike ICR, its sole purpose is to investigate crimes – so I was optimistic that things would be very different to my time on response.

I was immensely pleased that in PCT people were far more welcoming than they had been in ICR. There was no hazing, and I was offered tea instead of being expected to make it for everyone simply because I was new. My tutor in PCT was another great guy, who we'll call Ali. He was a very diligent, calm and considered officer. He was also the first officer who was able to answer my questions about police processes and various scenarios in a considered manner. It was a world apart from ICR, and I was elated.

That said, PCT struggled with many of the same things other departments suffered with – namely a high turnover and critically low levels of staffing. For instance, most teams in PCT were supposed to be around four to five people, led by a sergeant. At least one of the teams during my time there had just one DC and one sergeant.

In Slough, PCT dealt only with burglaries and robberies – which were a frequent occurrence. We dealt with all types of burglaries: commercial burglaries, dwelling burglaries, 'vamoose burglaries' (where the offenders gained entry to the house to steal car keys and then stole the car), and... shit burglaries.

"What is a shit burglary?" I asked Ali with a laugh when he first used the term.

"You'll find out soon enough," he replied with a smile.

At the time, I thought this must be a sign of how jaded the officers were after having worked in the police for so many years. I never thought burglaries could be seen as shitty jobs by officers. It's a serious crime!

I soon found out what they meant. An early case I dealt with involved a man in his 50s living in a supported housing establishment, who had accused the staff of stealing money from his room. This wasn't an emergency, so we didn't head over on blues – we made an appointment and drove over to investigate.

I entered the man's room; it was a tip. It was the type of room where you have to look hard for spots on the floor to step that aren't covered in junk. The female member of staff who met us said that they'd offered to help him clean, but he didn't want them in his room. Having negotiated my way across the floor, I started to talk to the man, who was lying topless on his bed, belly hanging over the edge of the mattress. I started with this business of not having the staff in his room.

"Nah, I don't want them in here," he confirmed. "You see what they do. They take my money."

I asked him what made him so sure it was the staff. He said he wouldn't suspect any of the other residents so it had to be the staff.

As I questioned him further, he told me that the money that had gone missing was bills of cash rolled up inside a handbag. He took the handbag out with him when he went to the shops. Yesterday, he'd gone to the shops to buy alcohol, and had drunk five or six cans of beer in his room. The next day he'd realised his money was gone.

The staff member confirmed his story, and said he was drinking heavily. She told us that the man had been repeatedly warned not to smoke marijuana on the premises and had ignored those warnings, and was at risk of being evicted from the establishment; she suspected that he held a grudge towards staff because of this.

I strongly suspected that the man had simply spent the money and forgotten about it. However, as we've already said, you can't just rely on your gut feeling – you have to investigate. But there were no reasonable lines of enquiry to follow. There were no witnesses, there was no CCTV, and so there was no way to investigate this particular case. All we had was two conflicting stories, and no way to establish which was true – and in the end, we took no further action.

A week later he called again with exactly the same allegation.

It wasn't long before I started to talk about shit burglaries too. Especially since we still had to go through the process every time a crime was reported – all the statements, all the paperwork – knowing that we'd be able to do nothing about it.

This was part of the central paradox of PCT. At TVP, and in policing in general, our priorities were crimes involving violence against women, sexual offences, organised crime, terrorism – you know, the big crimes. Yet here we were in the Priority Crime Team, dealing with burglaries – lots of which never really went anywhere. The truth was that burglaries and robberies were considered volume crime, although slightly too much work for patrol officers, so PCT was set up to handle them. I suppose it was an operational priority – we had lots of robberies and burglaries to deal with, so a team was created specifically for the job – but unfortunately, as we'll get into, we didn't often get the resources that you'd think a team with 'priority' in the name should have. And, as I've said, we were chronically understaffed.

You might be wondering what happened to crimes that were even less of a priority. There was another team for those crimes: the Smart Resolution Team. This was essentially a jazzy name for a proverbial bin. If a case was sent to the Smart Resolution Team it was essentially being binned off. Crimes reported online that weren't serious - such as bike thefts – would be handled by the Smart Resolution Team.

So, I started to get settled into PCT. The shifts were much better – mainly because there were no night shifts. There were early shifts (07:00-16:00) or late shifts (14:00-22:00). The shift pattern, though, was a bit strange. Sometimes I'd do three days in a row, other times five, other times two. Sometimes I would have two rest days in a row, sometimes three.

I got to know our sergeant, Peter, who was a lovely and supportive manager. He never seemed to get tired, and managed to live off a single packet of Super Noodles on an evening shift. As time went on, I wondered where his body got the fuel to manage those shifts.

A memorable moment was a burglary in an AirBnB. It was my first time attending a burglary and I was the joint OIC with Ali. A family was staying in the AirBnB temporarily while looking for a more permanent home, having recently moved to the UK. Some youths had broken in through the window, and had actually been seen by the father of the family as they arrived home – he'd even given chase for a while. Luckily for the family, the only thing stolen had been cigarettes – the burglars had left a laptop and various expensive electronic devices.

"That happens a lot these days," Ali told me. "With the passwords and security on electronics they're harder to fence; you can sell cigarettes on easy."

I was really keen to investigate this, as you might expect. I had a look around the property for physical evidence, which proved fruitless. However, I did see a CCTV camera that looked like it was covering the back of the house, and would therefore have given us a great view of the suspects. I decided to try and get hold of it.

"Leave it for now," Ali told me, "we'll make a note and the investigation support officers will do that bit." Investigation support officers are, as the name implies, there to support an investigation from an admin perspective – taking witness statements in some cases, gathering evidence, and so on. So, I noted the CCTV on the system and sent a task through the system to the investigation support officers.

Two weeks later, I'd heard nothing. I checked in with the investigation support officers; they'd not had time to go and get the CCTV. So I chased it up myself, only to discover that the footage from the night in question had been overwritten to make way for newer footage. I didn't make a big fuss to Ali and the others – and Ali, for his part, didn't seem at all surprised at the way it had gone down, or particularly bothered. But inside I was furious that we'd lost potentially vital evidence for the case. I decided from then on that if I needed something done on my investigation, I'd have to do it myself. I couldn't leave it to the investigation support officers, who could always fall back on the excuse of not enough time and not enough manpower. Unfortunately, it wasn't the last time I'd be let down by bureaucracy in my time at PCT.

Finally, alongside this work I still had my case from ICR involving the man who had assaulted the NHS staff at Wexham Park. I felt strongly enough about this case that I asked specifically to keep it with me when I moved; I also thought it would be a great learning experience for me to see a case through all the way to the end. Plus, I'd personally met and spoken with the victims and the witnesses; I wanted to give them consistency in the case.

CHAPTER 15

THE VICTIM-OFFENDER SPECTRUM

'Victims are at the heart of everything we do.'

'Victim-led.'

'Victim-focussed.'

There's no buzzword in policing like the word 'victim'. You'll never find a UK policing strategy that doesn't include a phrase around putting victims first or prioritising victims of crime. And obviously, victims are hugely important. They can go through very traumatic experiences during a crime, and in the aftermath, and it's right that the police take steps to look after the victims of crime. How that translated into reality, though, was complex – especially in PCT.

To try and improve victim satisfactions rates, and to tightly monitor victim contact, TVP introduced the victim contact contract (VCC). It was introduced largely because victims often felt they were left in the dark by the police regarding the progress or outcome of their case. So, for every case, you have to draft a VCC in which you agree with the victim how often you'll update them. To ensure that we were keeping up with our obligations under the VCC, all victim contact had to be logged – if it wasn't logged, it didn't count. The presence of VCCs on cases was regularly checked by senior officers, as was the actual victim contact that took place.

I remember a time in ICR that my sergeant approached me.

"Jade, one of your occurrences is missing a VCC. Can you fix that, please?"

In case you're wondering what an 'occurrence' is, it's a specific crime. A 'case' can include multiple occurrences, each with their own crime report. For instance, my Wexham Park assault suspect had one case with multiple occurrences in it because there were multiple victims. You had one occurrence for each victim, all part of the same case.

I looked through all my occurrences on Niche, and they all had a VCC.

"I don't know which one you're referring to, sorry," I told my sergeant.

"The one ending -354," she replied. I opened up the occurrence. It was a criminal damage offence against a police van. The suspect, detained in the back of the van, had decided to spit all over the glass screen.

"Thames Valley Police is the victim in that occurrence. Surely the police force itself doesn't require contact or updates?" I asked.

"Oh right," my sergeant responded, "that's fine. Just put a VCC in anyway and leave it blank. At least it will show up on the figures as complete."

I did it, of course. Middle management is under pressure from higher management to get VCC figures up, which trickles down into pressure on regular officers to get a VCC for every single case. But this sort of bureaucracy has always annoyed me. VCC percentages seemed to be the main concern for managers most days. Why? So they can show off good figures in PowerPoint presentations to their seniors. 'Look how good our victim contact is. 95% of victims were contacted every 30 days about their case.' If you can show that under your leadership these figures improved you have a strong case for promotion.

My problem with it is that in the relentless drive for VCCs, the purpose of them was being forgotten. Sometimes that manifested itself in nonsensical VCCs like the one I created for the police van crime. But it could easily have been us trying to contact people who didn't want to be contacted – which could have caused more harm than good.

And, of course, simply creating and adhering to a VCC doesn't really say anything about whether victims are actually satisfied with the contact they receive. In my experience, the VCC figures became a goal in themselves rather than actually contacting the victims behind those VCCs to their satisfaction.

Coming back to PCT more specifically, another important thing to remember when thinking about victims is that there is a huge overlap between victims and suspects. Remember those Slough jobs I mentioned earlier? We had loads of those in PCT. Although the fact that someone is also a well-known criminal never deterred us from investigating a case as fully as we could, it usually made it much trickier to investigate since the victim often didn't want anything to do with the police. Even if they made the initial call, after that the victim would never answer the phone again, or open their door to you. It was quite common that they would give us fake numbers to call to stop us contacting them. Despite all this, however, we had to keep trying because we had an active investigation to pursue.

A great example of a Slough job from my time in PCT took place one Saturday night. Late in the evening there was a call from the control room about a new robbery case. A man with a sports bag full of cash was walking from his car to his house, carrying the bag. On his doorstep, someone threatened him with a machete and took the bag off him.

It was a straightforward robbery, but you may be wondering: why did the victim have a sports bag full of cash?

This was an example of a very typical crime that took place between criminals – one robbing another of the profits of their own criminal activities. I can't remember how the police became involved in this particular crime, but it wouldn't surprise me if it had been a witness reporting it rather than the victim themselves. But reported it was, so we had to attempt to make contact and investigate.

We spoke to the victim of the robbery over the phone very briefly. He said he was going on holiday tomorrow so he couldn't be reached.

"I'll sort it out myself once I get back," he said.

It was plain as day that he didn't want police involved, but unfortunately for him it was too late for that. As per our own guidelines, we kept chasing him for weeks as we received repeated instructions from Niche to take a victim statement, refer him to victim services, and complete a VCC – all standard actions that have to be carried out with all victims of crime. It all came to naught.

Typically, it was extremely hard to close cases like this, even if you knew for certain that no robbery charge would ever come out of it and that it was taking time away from other crimes that stood a better chance of getting a charge. What usually happened was that, once you'd exhausted all your lines of enquiry and had no response from the victim for a certain period of time, your sergeant would close the case and write up a rationale for why it was being closed with so little progress.

So, we have an environment where victims have to be prioritised, but where the way that happens is a bit bureaucratic and soulless. And the picture is complicated by the fact that many victims were also criminals themselves. Unfortunately, my experience of the system was that it's not well-equipped to handle those nuances.

When dealing with incidents in any police department the first thing that needs to be established is who is the victim and who is the suspect? That's because, on Niche, you have to pick a victim and suspect (or multiple suspects) for each case. Often, this is straightforward. Let's say person A hits person B. Person A is the suspect of assault, person B the victim.

Although from a data recording perspective this makes sense, I was surprised at how quickly involved persons are put into categories that can lead to some bias. You see a record with one person as the victim, and one as the suspect. You're automatically more likely to feel supportive towards the victim, and more suspicious of the suspect. Investigators are supposed to do their job completely without bias – you're not trying to prove someone guilty or innocent, but to get to the truth of an incident. But, whether you want to or not, whether you've received critical thinking and bias training or not, the categories people are put into on the system will influence how you think and behave with them – particularly since there are separate procedures for victims and suspects.

Of course, there's always the chance too that your initial recording of these categories was incorrect. It might later turn out that person B actually hit person A, making your suspect the victim and the victim a suspect. From a case management perspective the fix was simple – you'd close the case and open a new one with the correct victim and suspect. But depending on how long it took for that information to come to light, how much damage had been done because of the way we had to categorise people?

Even the idle chat around the water cooler could help reinforce biases. Although we never took anything said in interviews at face value, and never relied on our gut instincts, a popular conversation on a break was to discuss who you believed in whatever cases were ongoing at the moment. On one level it was harmless small talk that is inevitable in a police station, but on another level it likely reinforced unconscious biases. It's only natural to talk about it when you're working in the police – but it shows just how hard it is to maintain true impartiality.

In reality, the situation is much more complex than a victim and a suspect. As we've said, many suspects are also victims and many victims suspects. Sometimes at the same time. There's the example above with the sports bag full of cash, where one criminal commits a crime against another. But there are other, more nuanced examples. Think of a person struggling with substance misuse issues, for instance. Their addiction may cause them to often commit theft or public order offences, but their vulnerability and the circles they move in will also make them frequent victims of assault or theft themselves. People involved in gangs are likely to be the perpetrators and the victims of serious violent crimes. Child gang members may be dealing drugs and carrying weapons, but at the same time be victims of exploitation and grooming.

In a world where the victim and offender are seen as polar opposites and distinct categories, I think it's hard for anyone – even the police – to conceptualise that someone can be both.

Thinking more about gangs, even if you consider (and the police are encouraged to do this) that children dealing drugs for gangs are not offenders but victims of exploitation and trafficking, what happens when they turn 18? Are they still victims? What about when they turn 24 and they're now heavily embedded in drug dealing, violence and grooming others? They're an adult, and legally responsible for their own actions so we may start to view them more as purely an offender now. But they're an adult who's been shaped by their experiences as a child. Are they a victim? An offender? Or both?

As if that wasn't enough, sometimes it's even unclear in a given situation who the victim and suspect are. At training, we spent a day doing several domestic abuse roleplay scenarios. Two officers from the group would engage in the role play and then the class would discuss the scenario. One of the scenarios was as follows: the police had been called to an address by neighbours after they heard shouting. When the police arrived, they found a husband

and wife in a heated argument. The police spoke to both of them and found out that they'd been arguing over finances. The husband worked full-time and was the sole breadwinner, while the wife managed the household. The argument had begun after the wife had bought new shoes for herself; the husband got angry because he believed this was a waste of money and that they should be spending their money more wisely. The wife thought it was her right to treat herself once in a while. After further questioning there were no indications of domestic abuse of any kind.

"So, who's the victim?" asked the trainer.

"There is no victim," someone piped up. He shook his head.

"It's a domestic case. You have to decide who you are going to record as the victim and who you are going to do the DOM5 with." (That's the domestic abuse risk assessment, remember.)

I was puzzled. Who is the victim in this case? Couldn't we just put both people down as 'involved' rather than victims or suspects? The answer was no. You had to maintain the strict dichotomy. One person had to be the victim, one (or more) the suspect. The trainer told us that the wife in this case was the 'suspect' and the husband the 'victim' as the wife's behaviour had caused the current argument.

I disagreed, of course. Dan's interpretation was wildly different from mine. You could argue that the husband overreacted to a trivial thing and that he in fact instigated the argument. You could even argue that there was a risk of financial abuse going on, since the husband was trying to exert control over their finances.

"Isn't it going to bias officers in the future if they attend the address?" I asked. "The control room will likely tell them there's been a previous incident where the husband was the victim."

"Well," he replied, "if you let that affect you, you're not doing a good job."

An admirable sentiment, but I know a little about the psychology of bias. For instance, that you can't just switch it off.

I can't really see a solution, sadly. Labelling people as 'involved' and then building context around that until you can make an informed decision about who is a victim and who is a suspect is not feasible in the current criminal justice system. It would pretty much require a complete overhaul of the legal system. From a legal perspective it makes complete sense to have this strict victim-offender dichotomy, so that cases can be tried in a consistent manner and justice can be dispensed at scale. But this dichotomy felt strange to me, and only felt stranger as I gained more experience as an officer and saw the realities of the victim-offender spectrum for myself. And believing that our investigative training will protect us from such bias, I think, is naïve.

CHAPTER 16

SETTLING INTO PCT

While ICR work had been very reactive, on-the-go, and high-adrenaline, PCT was very process-based. You were handed a case, and there was a specific series of steps to take to complete it. Note that I said 'complete', not 'solve' – after all, lots of cases never get solved even though you pursue all reasonable lines of enquiry and have done all you can do.

I felt like I could be good at this kind of work – it was calmer and more considered, requiring you to sit and think about things for a while before taking action.

I suppose that at this point I was officially doing 'detective' work and so could start thinking of myself as a detective. In fact, I got to start signing my emails 'TDC' for 'Trainee Detective Constable'. Looking back, though, I didn't really mark that moment, or feel that elation that I'd felt when I joined Sully. My existence was very much day-to-day; even though the work was less intense than ICR, the different style of work meant that in many ways I was starting from zero again.

I can't honestly say that my training at Sully prepared me any better for PCT than it did for ICR. I already mentioned that we still had assignments to complete after our initial training; we also had study weeks to get through. The study weeks were essentially back to back online lectures, which we attended from home over Teams. Any enjoyment we might have felt at being off work to learn was quickly overtaken by the mind-numbing boredom of what we were covering. But just like our initial training, much of what we were learning in our study weeks felt almost completely unrelated to our day-to-day work.

To show you what I mean, most of what we did in PCT was preparing case files. At Sully, we spent a total of two days on the topic. Those two days had been spent in presentations that took you through all the paperwork, but since we had no real context it was very hard to follow. On top of that, our trainers didn't have in-depth knowledge of casefiles. Some of them hadn't been involved in detective work and so didn't have much experience, and those that did told us that everything had changed since their day. And our study weeks didn't cover anything to do with case files either.

All this meant that when I actually got into the work in PCT, I was working so hard mentally – and still recovering physically from my time in ICR – that any excitement I might have felt about my situation was washed away. On top of that, PCT was quite different to what I'd thought investigating might look like. Even after Sully, in my head investigations seemed to me to be a relatively creative field – using your brain to wrap your head around a situation, investigate the right areas, find the evidence, solve the crime. PCT, as I've said, was a lot more process-based – largely, I suspect, because we were dealing with the same kind of volume crime every day. Not as exciting as I'd hoped, but fine. Except, the process we had to follow was often hampered by a lack of resources. For example: if you wanted to get forensic analysis done, you'd have to apply. If they didn't think you had a good chance of getting a charge or a conviction, they would turn you down. A colleague from my time in CID once told me she believed every case could be solved if you got enough resources. She may well have been right, but the only cases that tended to get lots of resources thrown at them were murder, terrorism and perhaps organised crime – and those weren't what PCT dealt with.

There were a lot of long and late nights in PCT; though I never got close to the levels of exhaustion I felt in ICR, I still felt extremely fatigued by the work. The late nights happened when a call came in near the end of a shift – a 9.30pm call when you're due to finish at 10pm, for instance. Those calls would fill everyone with dread, and often people sought for excuses not to pick up – though of course, someone always did. A live case coming in at that point into your shift could mean serious overtime – you could spend the whole night in the station if you were on a late shift. Since there was no night shift in PCT, it was generally frowned upon to leave a case overnight if you could make progress on it. Peter the sergeant seemed to hardly tire at all during these long night shifts and could still make small talk and smile. I definitely could not, even though I would often bring in a home-cooked meal while he would subsist on those Super Noodles.

Building on that theme of looking for excuses, I discovered quite quickly that every department is always trying to dodge responsibility for a case. Not, I should add, because they don't care – but because almost every department is overworked and overstretched. When resources are so tight, the sergeants and inspectors battled over who should take ownership of investigations to try and protect their people.

In PCT, we only dealt with burglaries and robberies. The phrases "that's not a burglary, that's a theft in a dwelling" and "that's not a robbery, that's an assault and theft" became a standing joke. Though, of course, we did want to keep our caseload manageable – so if something genuinely wasn't a burglary or a robbery, we would get rid of it with lightning speed.

Since I can tell you're curious, let's go over the difference between burglaries, robberies, thefts in dwellings, and assaults and thefts quickly. To paraphrase the law, a burglary is defined in UK law as having entered a property (or part of a property) as a trespasser, and stealing property or inflicting grievous bodily harm (GBH) on someone – or attempting to do so. It also counts as a burglary if you enter as a trespasser with the intent to steal or inflict GBH, even if you don't do so. So, if you broke into my house and took my phone, that would be a burglary. However, if I invited you into my living room and later on you decided you wanted to steal my phone from the coffee table, that would NOT be a burglary – that would be a theft in a dwelling. But, if I invited you into my living room, and then you went into my bedroom to steal my phone, that WOULD be a burglary because even though I invited you into my house, you're trespassing in my bedroom because I didn't give you permission to enter there. It would still be a burglary even if you didn't actually take anything – because you've gone into my room intending to steal, that's enough to be charged with burglary.

Robbery occurs when someone steals something and, either just before or during the act, uses force on a person or threatens them with immediate harm. So if we met in the street, I knocked you out in order to go through your pockets, and take your wallet, that's robbery. However, if we met in the street, I knocked you out because we had a fight about something else, your wallet fell out of your pocket, and I took it, that would be an assault and theft because I didn't use force in order to take your wallet.

By the by, the act of stealing requires a person to take something they know they don't have the right to deprive someone of. For instance, there was a case in 1967 where a person drew a knife on their employer, demanding their wages. The wages in question were not due for a few days, but the person genuinely thought that they were – so from their perspective they had the right in law to take the money from their employer. Because of this, the case wasn't a theft, or a robbery (though there would almost certainly have been some other charge that could have been brought). For this reason, police have to think carefully about which offences are present in a case. If, for instance, someone is charged with burglary but their defence can prove it wasn't a burglary because the thief hadn't trespassed, then your entire case could get thrown out.

As well as trying to get rid of cases based on what crime was committed, everyone jumped at the opportunity to pass off jobs to other police forces. Did the crime happen in their area? Well, they'll need to investigate and interview the suspect. I suspect that every police department got passed as many jobs in this way as they managed to get rid of, but since every department did it, there was no point in stopping – you'd just end up with more cases that way!

Of course, once a job was definitely in your team, then everyone took ownership and worked hard to get the work done, i's dotted and t's crossed. But the mental gymnastics people went through before that… man, did people try and dodge it!

Alongside my PCT workload, I also had my Wexham Park case to progress. There was lots of paperwork to do for that, as well as the duty of keeping the victims and witnesses informed of my progress on the case. I bugged Ali relentlessly for help with this case, and I'll always be grateful that he helped me with it.

CHAPTER 17

MORE INVESTIGATIONS AND CHIS

Though Slough jobs were often dead-end and frustrating jobs, on occasion they turned out to be fascinating. Whilst working in PCT, I attended a burglary where the victim was an individual known to the police as a prolific, low-level street criminal. Given that he was frequently a suspect in other cases, he was a surprisingly decent, nice guy when I was dealing with him – though I wasn't the OIC, I was there to take the statement and assess the crime scene.

Inside his house, it was obvious that someone had broken in with a view to steal something. It was a tip. Cupboards had been emptied, drawers pulled out, and so on. However, the items that our victim reported stolen were going to be very hard to trace. I remember one of the items reported stolen was 'a bunch of £20 notes that were in the bottom of this box.' Say what you will about bank fraud and digital theft, but I'd rather trace money that's been stolen online instead of cash any day.

Anyway, despite the challenges with the case, I got on with taking a statement and asking CSI to come and investigate the scene. But the whole time I was with the victim, he was on the phone talking to someone. It was a little frustrating trying to get his statement, but generally speaking you have to be accommodating to someone who's just been the victim of a crime.

Eventually, he hangs up from his call.

"I know who did it," he announced. I was surprised, obviously.

"Um, OK," I replied, "who?"

The victim gave me a name that he'd got from his network of fellow street criminals. And sure enough, as we went through the CCTV from the scene and gathered more evidence, it turned out to be exactly who he said it was. I think we even got a charge out of the case. I remember being fascinated that his network of street criminals had been able to turn up the right name, and faster than the police would have got to it. They say there's no honour among thieves, but I think that it might be more that honour between thieves is a very fickle and situational thing.

That story seems like a good place to talk a bit about one of those sexy topics in crime dramas – the use of informants. On the telly, informants seem to be forever springing up with titbits for the police that help them crack the case. In the departments where I worked the use of informants was rare. The technical name for an informant is a CHIS: a covert human intelligence source. That could include criminal informants, members of the public such as the neighbours of a suspect, and undercover officers who interact with suspects – though those are rare. Given the risk to all involved, the use of a CHIS tended to be limited to more serious cases, and the information was kept very much confidential.

The situation in which an individual classes as a CHIS is quite specific as well. Our burglary victim, for instance, was not a CHIS because we hadn't tasked him to obtain specific information for us – he simply volunteered the information. Similarly, at another point during my time in PCT, Ali and I were driving a guy home after interviewing him in connection with drug possession and burglary. Ali casually asked him whether the gangs in the area were still using the same old lines from the year before ('lines' in this context being dedicated phone lines for drug dealing– you might be familiar with the term used in the phrase 'county lines' as it crops up in the news fairly often). To my great surprise, the suspect gave us an answer that was quite useful. However, because we didn't actually ask the suspect to find out a specific piece of information for us, he wouldn't have counted as a CHIS. Regardless, it struck me at the time as a cool bit of investigative work on Ali's part.

Anyway, aside from some of the more memorable investigations, my time in PCT continued to be an exhausting slog of paperwork and late nights, made bearable by the people I worked with. In some ways, I came to feel that solving a case wasn't up to me. My job was to follow the procedures of the job, and if a case was solvable with the resources we had available, it would be. I suppose that makes sense in a way – the process enables more people to solve more cases, rather than relying on an individual's intelligence or genius for problem-solving – but it didn't feel terribly rewarding or exciting.

I remember early on in my time at PCT I was chatting with the Chief Inspector and some others. The Chief Inspector asked me:

"So, do you like it here? Did you expect the work to be like this?"

"Um, yes, I guess so," I spluttered. Truth be told, I hadn't given it much thought at the time. As I said before, at this time in my life I was still living day by day. My brain was so occupied with trying to learn the ropes in my department and get competent at my job that I hadn't given much thought to how I enjoyed the work. Thinking on a wider level about my experience with the police, I didn't feel like that particular conversation was the time or place to give the CI a proper answer to her question – it was an off-the-cuff remark in a group conversation. I certainly didn't want to be burning bridges this early in my career, or clueing in the other officers in the conversation to the fact that I was having doubts about the wisdom of my decision to become a detective. Which, looking back, I can see plainly was what lay at the heart of some of my emotions during that time, even though I couldn't see it then. I was still keen to fight for the job I'd worked so hard to get, and to do my best to make it a success, even as the realities of the job continued to disconcert me at every turn.

CHAPTER 18

COURT

As part of my experience in PCT, my sergeant and I agreed it would be good to attend Crown court at least once to observe what happened during a trial. So I accompanied Ali to a robbery case which had gone to trial. The case in question was between a defendant who had beaten the plaintiff and subsequently taken money from him. It personally sounded like an assault and a theft to me, but it seemed a bit late to point that out.

The plaintiff alleged the defendant had attacked him out of the blue. The defendant alleged she'd acted in self-defence after the plaintiff had come on to her. I'd read the casefiles before going to court, and I'd seen the defendant on numerous briefing slides in connection with violent offences. She had about 300 records on Niche, including assaulting police officers and members of the public, and other officers had told me that she's been extremely violent upon arrest. So I admit that I was inclined to believe the plaintiff's version of events. He had no previous convictions, but he was homeless and had alcohol addiction issues.

I went to Reading Crown Court to observe during two days of the trial. On the first day I attended, the defendant did not show up. The excuse given was that she wasn't feeling well. To my surprise, the judge decided not to relay this information to the jury. Instead, he simply told them the defendant 'could not be here today' and that the jury should not hold this against her. In case you're not familiar with how court works, the judge, jury and barristers are not all closeted together for the entirety of the trial. Often the jury is dismissed so that the judge and barristers can decide what will be presented to the jury.

I remember thinking to myself: how easy was it to escape your day in court as a robbery defendant? And mess everyone about, costing public services a lot of time and money in the process?

Another thing that surprised me during the trial was that the court (meaning the judge and the jury) was not allowed to draw any adverse inferences. If you want the full detail about adverse inferences, you should read sections 34 – 37 of Criminal Justice and Public Order Act 1994 – but in general terms, an adverse inference comes about in a few situations:

- A defendant fails to mention facts when questioned or charged that they later present in court as part of their defence.
- A defendant maintaining silence at their trial.
- A defendant fails to explain the presence of objects, substances, or marks – like fingerprints – found on their person or in their possession.
- A defendant's refusal or failure to account for his or her presence at the location where an offence took place.

Essentially, if any of those things happen, normally the court is allowed to take this into consideration and question why the defendant did this. When the police arrest you in the UK, they have to warn you about this when they read you a caution which includes the phrase:

"You do not have to say anything. But, it may harm your defence if you do not mention when questioned something which you later rely on in court."

In this trial, an adverse inference could have been drawn because the defendant had given a 'no comment' interview – so she had failed to mention that story, and was now relying on it in court. However, the decision was made by the court not to allow an adverse inference to be drawn. The reason was that the woman was considered vulnerable. I didn't know her full history, but I do know she was diagnosed with ADHD.

During the trial while the jury and judge were in the room, the defendant presented as meek and shy. She had a fiddly toy in her hand, which was apparently to help with her concentration due to her ADHD, which she played with constantly while answering questions from the barristers. The barristers had received instructions not to ask her difficult questions as she might not understand, and as a result she was treated much like a 7 year-old child would be. She looked down and gave her answers quietly.

All well and good, but as soon as the judge and jury left the room for a break, her demeanour changed like night and day. She tossed the toy to the side and looked over at her friends sitting in the audience. She smiled at them with something that seemed to me like malice, and started shouting over at them and laughing. I'm no mental health expert, but the transformation seemed so stark that I couldn't escape the feeling that she was putting on an act for the jury.

Ultimately, she was found not guilty by the jury.

I came away from the trial feeling sad and disillusioned in the justice system. Whatever the truth of this particular incident, the woman in question was free once more, with no indication that her history of terrorising her community and committing violent crime was about to change. And based on the performances I'd seen during the trial, it felt like the whole processes was, in a way, rigged. Trials are less about truth or justice but about who can craft the best story – who can play into the expectations and biases of a jury, who can manipulate the letter of the law in their favour.

The other side of court, which PCT gave me plenty of experience of, was preparing casefiles for court. These were the forms that many of our tutors in Sully essentially knew nothing about. Though the paperwork was thankfully digital, there was a mountain of it for every case. And it was a laborious process, where much of the information needed on each form was the same, but there was no way to copy and paste information between forms. Barely any information was automatically populated from Niche, which felt extremely illogical to me, and in the beginning it was pretty difficult to work out which forms were needed for each case, or even what sections of each form needed filling in. Oddly, the way it tended to work was that people became competent at different types of forms, instead of getting good at all the paperwork for a case. In some ways this made sense, and since there was a team of us working on things together it didn't hold us up too much. But it definitely frustrated my desire to be as competent as possible, as quickly as possible.

You also often needed sergeants or other seniors offers to sign your documents. A case in point – towards the end of my time in PCT, I was due to take a holiday and the paperwork for my Wexham Park Assault case was complete. All that was needed was a sergeant's review. The deadline for filing the case with the CPS was fast-approaching; summary offences like the ones we were charging the suspect with need to be submitted within six months, or the case would be dropped. Having spent quite a bit of time talking to the victims and witnesses – not to mention the hours and hours spent on the paperwork – I was dreading the prospect of the case being dropped because of admin delay. I begged the sergeant to review my paperwork while I was away on holiday – and luckily when I returned the paperwork had been signed and the casefile submitted. That felt great; one step closer to getting this guy convicted.

One final thing about the court experience that I found quite unsettling was the seeming lack of security. There is some security inside the court – most of them have metal detectors that you have to walk through to get in, for instance – but I wondered how quickly security would arrive if a defendant became violent during a trial. And as soon as you step outside the court building there is no security at all. I couldn't help thinking: 'what's stopping someone from waiting around the corner for me, a victim, or a witness involved in this case?' The answer is: nothing. If you wanted to assault or intimidate anyone involved in your case, you'd know exactly when and where they would be – it would be an ideal time to do it.

I once attended Magistrates court in Reading. As I passed through security, a man standing in the corridor looked at me.

"You're that officer from Slough, aren't you?"

I looked at him closely, but I didn't recognise him at all.

"You don't remember me, do you?" he said.

"I'm afraid not," I said to him, desperately trying to assess whether our interaction had been good or bad based on the conversation alone.

"Really?!" he exclaimed. I apologised and told him I had to get to my court room.

Later, when I left the court, he was still in the hallway.

"See you later," he said as I walked out.

I don't even really remember whether he seemed threatening, genial, or somewhere in between. But in that moment, I had no idea whether he was someone I arrested, a witness, or a victim – and he hadn't felt the need to enlighten me in our brief conversation. And it was fresh in my mind that outside court was an ideal time to jump someone as there was no security. It's entirely possible that 'see you later' was a completely innocent way of bidding me goodbye, but in my head it spiralled into something far more ominous. As I made my way through the busier part of Reading, I looked over my shoulder frequently to see if anyone was following me. Soon, I found that my walk had morphed into a light jog as I fled to the train station. I was a bit spooked.

Thankfully, on the train home I felt at ease again – but it really reinforced the idea in my head that court can be a dangerous place – even for a police officer involved in a case.

And then, one day, about three months into my time at PCT, Ali announced to the team that he'd got a new role and would be leaving the team.

We were happy for him, but it meant that our team in PCT would comprise one sergeant, one DC, one civilian investigator, and one trainee – me. The DC on the team wasn't yet experienced enough to be a tutor, and the civilian investigator wasn't qualified either – so I would be left without a tutor. This wasn't an unusual occurrence; though we were supposed to have a tutor in every rotation, staffing shortages meant that it was relatively common for a trainee to not have a tutor. I was going to miss Ali, though – he had looked after me well.

So, I was given the option of staying in PCT without a tutor, or of moving on to the Criminal Investigation Department (CID) where I would get a new tutor. I chose the latter – and looking back, I think that was a mistake.

My rationale was that I still felt like I needed the support of a tutor. Though PCT went at a slower and more considered pace than ICR, which suited my learning style better, there was so much to learn (I later discovered that various things I learned in PCT were wrong – but we'll get to that later). So I thought that moving to CID was the right call.

But despite its frustrations, I had enjoyed my time in PCT. The work suited me better than ICR had, and I was starting to get to grips with the job. Although it was more procedural than I'd expected, I was solving crimes. At Ali's urging, I'd even stopped using the 'T' from my title of 'TDC' and started calling myself a detective. I didn't really want to move on from PCT at all – but the issue of having a tutor drove me to the decision. And, as you'll see, CID was destined to be far and away the most challenging thing I'd ever done. It would push me to – and over – my limits, and ultimately be the beginning of my exit from the police.

PART 4

CRIMINAL INVESTIGATION DEPARTMENT

CHAPTER 19

WELCOME TO CID

The Criminal Investigation Department, or CID, investigates a different type of crime compared to PCT. While PCT was set up to investigate specific types of volume crime, CID is the traditional home of detectives in any police force. CIDs investigate serious assaults, rapes, serious sexual offences and other cases which are too serious and complex to be investigated by uniform officers.

The CID at Slough was the department where I saw most colleagues cry. The seriousness of the work, the workload, the hours – it all got on top of everyone sooner or later. In our team of eight – one sergeant, who we'll call Fara, five DCs, one civilian investigator, and me – I remember seeing at least five of my teammates cry in the office at various stages. For the longest time, I thought sergeant Fara – a calm, calculated woman who was good at her job and a very experienced police officer – was the only one who didn't let the work get to her. She often came across as cold, and I wondered if she was so jaded after her time in the police that she was incapable of any type of emotion. Then one day I finally saw her walk to the toilets in tears.

If I passed my two-year probation, CID was where I would most likely end up.

Speaking of that probation, by now I had been on the payroll at the police for almost a year – halfway through my probation and the DC DHEP course. Despite nearly a year's experience, the move to CID made me feel like I was starting from scratch yet again. Officially, after our training and our rotation in ICR, DC DHEP students like me were supposed to stay in PCT for the whole of their probation, apart from a rotation in the domestic abuse team in year two. In reality, we were often moved around based on the needs of our stations. Because of Ali's promotion, I was the first of my cohort to join CID – and it seemed that almost none of my previous knowledge was relevant in CID. I was also pretty nervous about the type of crime I'd be dealing with; was I really ready to be handling crimes like rape and GBH?

On reflection, the way the DC DHEP scheme was run did nothing for my confidence. Instead of doing some training and then putting it into practice, the scheme threw you in at the deep end – repeatedly. That just didn't gel with the way I learn things. I'm not exactly a perfectionist, but I don't want to learn through trial and error, especially when the stakes are so high. In each rotation I did at TVP, the pace was so fast and support so minimal that there was no alternative but to make mistakes and learn from them – whether those were with paperwork, handling a certain type of situation, or even just interacting with colleagues. And by the time I felt like I'd learned enough to stop making those mistakes, I'd be whisked off to a new department and I'd start again.

To extend the metaphor about being thrown in the deep end, by the time I joined CID I didn't feel like I was actually swimming, but I also hadn't drowned. I was still living day-to-day, getting through whatever was thrown at me and absorbing the stress from every misstep, lesson, or mishap that occurred. I was still keen to see the course through to the end, and I still wanted to be a detective at the end of it – but in the back of my mind, a seed of doubt was growing as to whether this was the right career for me.

My first day was very strange – when I arrived, there seemed to be about five times as many people in the building as there should be. Everyone was rushing about with lots of purpose, and most of them were people I'd never seen before. That was odd – after nearly a year, I was now familiar with most of the faces in the station.

I sat down at a desk and took out my laptop, and started looking for something to do – or someone to tell me what was going on. Eventually, I caught someone's eye.

"Hi," I said, "I'm Jade. It's my first day, I've just come over from PCT. Who should I report to?"

"Oh, right," my new colleague replied, "I'll find out who that is. We've got a murder on our hands, so Major Crime has taken over the CID. It's all a bit mental right now. Just wait there, OK?"

So, that explained it. We'll come on to the Major Crime Unit, or MCU, in a later chapter – but suffice to say for now that when a major crime is committed, the MCU takes over the investigation and can use all the department's resources – which they control very tightly.

After a little while, we were all called into a briefing. The details of the crime were explained, and everyone was given a role – except me, as the newbie.

In fact, in the early days of CID, when there was no live incident, there wasn't much for me to do. A live incident, from a CID perspective, is an incident that ICR has responded to and, due to the nature of the crime, has called CID in for. When that happened, we'd go down to the scene and start doing our work – making initial inquiries, getting statements from victims and witnesses, as well as interviewing anyone who had been arrested. Outside of those times, everyone else was doing paperwork or following up on cases already in progress – which I didn't have any of.

Though it kept the work from being too tiring initially, it was a bit lonely and contributed to my feeling of isolation. In PCT, Ali had always involved me in his casework to help me learn. I loved the learning, and the feeling of inclusion. At CID, nobody wanted help with their paperwork, despite my asking multiple times. I felt a bit uncomfortable being the only one who wasn't very busy – it felt a bit like not pulling my weight. I tried to rationalise it by telling myself that I'd soon get busy as I got assigned cases, and in the meantime I decided to do as much online training as possible. I remember that consisted of a few webinars about rape investigations, as well as a training package for an app called Pronto (which was essentially a digital pocket notebook).

Of course, with a new department came a new rota, just to keep me even further off-balance. While CID had the same early and late shifts as PCT – and no night shift, thank god – the rota had one seven-day working week every three weeks. In time, those seven-day stints would start to chip away at me.

My experience joining CID fell somewhere in the middle of my experiences at ICR and PCT. Nobody was unfriendly, which was nice, but they didn't go out of their way to introduce themselves. Sadly, one of the least friendly people was my new tutor. I've not bothered to come up with a name for her, because frankly our relationship barely got off the ground. After my experiences with Jay and Ali, this person was a real let down to me. After an initial meeting she barely acknowledged my presence most of the time; when we deployed to incidents, she usually chose to partner up with her friend in the team unless sergeant Fara ordered her to partner up with me. I was sure that, whenever I wasn't in the room, she was gossiping about me. On the few occasions we did interact, I got the feeling that she saw me as an annoying burden or a tickbox for her ongoing professional development.

I remember one case that she and I did attend together. A woman had reported a rape to us, and my tutor and I were sent to bring the woman into the station for an interview. We picked her up from her parents' house and once she was in the car, it quickly became apparent that something was off. Some of the things she said were very odd – completely disconnected from what was going on in the car. She would laugh at strange moments, even when nobody had said anything. She also kept referring to a 'they' in a slightly strange way. As we neared the station, I began to suspect that the woman was mentally unwell.

Once we were at the station, the interview commenced, with my tutor taking the lead. It wasn't an easy interview. The woman's story was relatively garbled, and seemed contradictory in some places. My tutor had to probe her multiple times from different angles to verify various elements of the story. What emerged eventually was that the victim had been taken advantage of by someone she met online. They slept together, and then he left.

Eventually, my tutor put down her pen.

"So what you're telling us is that you had consensual sex?" she said, irritation evident in her voice. "OK, we're taking you home."

It struck me as a very insensitive way to treat a potential victim. Even if her story didn't actually amount to an offence, the woman was very obviously distressed by what had happened – and, I suspect, was struggling with other issues that would affect her ability to provide informed consent in any case. The case certainly gave me misgivings about my new tutor.

In better news, very early on in my time at CID I heard back from the CPS. My Wexham Park assault suspect was being charged! It was my first ever charge as a police officer, and I was thrilled to have made it happen. We still had to wait for dates for a plea hearing, and either a sentencing hearing or a trial depending on how he pled – but we were on our way to it.

CHAPTER 20

SACCI

A few months into my time at CID, I was sent back to Sully for my Serious and Complex Interviewing (SACCI) course. This was a two-week advanced interview course specifically for detectives – an important part of my DC DHEP course. I was looking forward to having a break from Slough, but more than that I was very keen to learn more about interviewing. By this point in my career I'd done fewer than ten interviews, and even fewer as the lead interviewer. I'd heard so much conflicting information from colleagues about what to do and what not to do in interviews, and I was hoping to clear up those doubts during this course.

Being back at Sully was in many ways a balm. It felt like a holiday. There was no expectation to keep up to speed with your work back at your station, so I didn't have to respond to people in my evenings, or deal with the mental strain of the job. Even better, about half of my course mates from basic training were on the course too. Though the group WhatsApp chat was still there, it was essentially defunct by this point. Nobody messaged on there unless we all had a study week and people had questions about our course content. So it was great to see everyone, and the evenings were spent hanging out and catching up with each other.

In the months before the course, I had written a list of questions about interviewing; during the course, I slowly worked my way through the list. It became a running joke that at the end of every class (when everyone wanted to leave), I still had several questions to ask. I wouldn't be deterred from asking them, though. This was the environment in which I learned best, and perhaps my only opportunity to get clarity on topics that nobody could agree on back at the station. Plus, I really wanted to gain more confidence in the interview room before my next real interview.

I'm glad I did ask all my questions – because I realised during the course that many things I had copied from colleagues, or been told to do, were not actually correct procedures. For example, the lovely civilian investigator in PCT had never once written down what was said in a pre-interview briefing. But correct procedure is to capture it all. Part of me wondered why nobody had got in trouble over this – after all, not writing things down that were said was a breach of PACE. I can only assume that it went under the radar because PCT was dealing with volume crimes, so perhaps the level of scrutiny was less.

I had also been told, that in a 'no comment' interview you should just go through the questions in your interview plan one by one. 'Where were you yesterday morning?' 'Who were you with?' 'What time did you leave your house?' and so on. When I told my trainer this on the SACCI course, he winced.

"No, that's exactly what you should not be doing!" he said. "You should go topic by topic and make it fluid, conversational. Not read questions of a piece of paper like a robot."

In fairness to my colleagues, it's actually quite hard to make a 'no comment' interview conversational, for obvious reasons. But I understand the principle. The more fluid you can keep the conversation, the more information you're likely to get out of someone – even if they are in a 'no comment' frame of mind.

It's interesting to note that, in police films and series, the interview is often seen as a pivotal point in an investigation. Will the suspect talk? Will they let the one piece of information slip that blows the case wide open? Often the investigator is such a talented individual that the suspect begins talking, or confesses as the pressure finally gets them to crack. The real world is more mundane. In the real world, the interview is just one part of the procedure you follow when working a case, because the suspect has the right to give their account of what happened. A confession isn't enough to convict someone by itself. You still have to get evidence to corroborate the story, to reduce the chance that a suspect has made a false confession – which can happen due to coercion, mental illness, or even the suspect misunderstanding the charges against them.

But getting a confession is rare – in my time in the police, I only got one (we'll get to it in a bit). Amongst gangs and more prolific criminals there is an unwritten rule that regardless of the situation you'll always say 'no comment' in interview. Beyond being a metaphorical 'fuck you' to the police, 'going no comment' has a specific benefit. It allows you to assess what evidence the police has against you so far without pinning yourself down to one story. Then if the case goes to court, you can create a story that fits with the available evidence. As we discussed above, the risk of this approach is that the court will draw an adverse inference from your silence in interview – but as that story showed, it's not always a given.

The other path an interview can take is that the suspect will provide a prepared statement with the help of their solicitor or legal representative. This is usually a brief statement to say they had no involvement in the offence, after which the suspect answers 'no comment' to all questions.

Apart from being not much use to an investigator, the 'no comment' interviews are not very interesting or exciting. The interviews where someone gives an account are much more challenging and engaging. You never quite know what angle they're going to take, and sometimes their stories can take you by surprise. As the interviewer, you have to listen very carefully to their account, while simultaneously making notes, thinking of follow up questions, and thinking about whether the story fits with the evidence you already have. It's mentally quite a challenging task, and one I really enjoyed – it's just not quite the dramatic moment the TV would have you believe.

We also did some roleplays on the SACCI course. We each had to do an assessed roleplay as an interviewer, and we each took turns playing the role of suspects or witnesses for our course mates. It was quite fun – when playing victims or suspects, we were each given prompt sheets with details about our character and had to do our best to convincingly stay in character through the interview.

It was also very interesting to hear how my course mates had got on in their first year of policing. I hadn't seen any of them since training, and some of them I hadn't even spoken to since we graduated. Many of them had shared similar experiences to mine. The stress, the exhaustion, the frustration with how the system worked. In a way, I felt relieved about that – at least I wasn't the odd one out of the group. Everyone still professed that they were keen and had some excitement for their work, too. I'm not sure how much of that I believed. I learned early on that everyone kept up appearances – you'd never know if someone was struggling until they quit. Two of our course mates did just that. Whenever you'd see them or talk to them, everything sounded fine, and they seemed to be doing great as officers. Then, out of the blue, they both announced they hated the job and were quitting. So I didn't waste too much time comparing their levels of enthusiasm with my own.

CHAPTER 21

SETTING OFFICERS UP FOR SUCCESS

In many ways, the way a police station is run feels like it's designed to make it as hard as possible for you to do your job. In my experience, that comes from a few places. Some of the problems are down to years of underfunding. Some are due to the age of the facilities and systems we use. Others are down to the crushing bureaucracy that comes with any public sector job, and especially in the police. They weren't always anyone's fault (or not anyone's that I could identify, anyway) but they conspired to make everyone's life harder than it needed to be.

The first thing I noticed, way back when I was in ICR, was that even if you came in on time for your shift, it would be likely that all computer docking stations were full and there would be nowhere to plug in your laptop. Hell, sometimes there wouldn't even be a chair left. There just wasn't enough room for everyone. The result was that people came in earlier and earlier to try and secure a space – leading to longer working hours and, undoubtedly, more burnout.

Then there was the issue of parking. When I started working at Slough, I was advised to arrive one hour early for a late shift to secure parking. This was again an issue of capacity. There were only a few parking spaces at the front of the station, and a few at the back. If you did manage to get a space, you could guarantee that your car would be blocked in by someone else's car by the end of the shift. Sometimes the cars even went three deep. It meant that, at the end of your shift, you had to pray that the people blocking you in were either at the station, or had left their key at reception so you could move their car. If they didn't, you'd just have to wait until that person came back from wherever they were. Thankfully that never happened to me, but it was relatively common that people would end up staying an hour or more past the end of their shift, simply because they couldn't get their car out. Again, this was the best case scenario, which assumed you arrived about an hour early for your shift.

If you didn't want to add an hour on to the start of your day and risk adding on more to the end of it, you had some other options – none of them great. You could park in a nearby residential area, about fifteen minutes from the station, but we had several group emails sent telling us that officers' cars had been keyed when parked there.

You could pay for parking outside the station – but you could only stay there for three hours, after which you'd have to move the car. If you didn't (because you were out on patrol, for instance), then you'd just get fined. I don't know if anyone ever tried contesting those fines, but I doubt the council would waive them.

My preferred option on late shifts was a few free spaces that were about a 25 minute walk away from the station. It meant a walk across town in the dark at the end of a shift, but it was worth it to save the money and hassle. That's where I'd always try first. After that, for preference I'd dump the car near a building site close to the station or take the risk of paying for parking. If neither of those options worked, I'd take my chances on the residential estate where cars got scratched. Anything rather than parking in the police car park.

My main reasons for avoiding the police car park were that I couldn't stand the idea of turning up an hour early and risking staying an hour late, and that I always felt uncomfortable driving other people's cars. The few times I did it, I found myself sweating as I gingerly moved the cars around. They were crammed in so tight that it was a matter of inches that stood between a safe exit and scratching either your car, someone else's, or both. It was a whole lot of extra stress every day which I didn't really want. I saw another officer scratch a car one day.

"Oh balls," she sighed, "now I've got to find out whose that is."

On the other side of that equation, group emails came round relatively frequently from someone whose car had been scratched, imploring the culprit to own up.

My tutor in ICR, Jay, had decided long ago that he would park in the court bays. The magistrate's court is directly next to Slough police station, and the two shared a car park – with those bays reserved to try and protect some space for members of the court. I saw several angry emails from the station commander about not ever parking in the court bays; threats were made about banning certain people from the car park entirely if they don't obey this rule. Every time I saw Jay's car parked in a court bay after yet another all-user warning email, I couldn't help but smile.

The next topic is IT. I've talked extensively already about Niche, our case management system. It looked like it had been developed in the 90s for a completely different purpose than managing crime information. At Slough, Niche frequently crashed, deleting whatever you were working on, or failed to start. It regularly cost everyone a few hours of their day. In the end, I resorted to writing all my notes up in Word, where I could save them and recover them, and uploading them to Niche from there.

During my time in PCT, I discovered the two-way interface, or TWIF module of Niche and with it a new level of hatred for the system. TWIF is a method of sending documents to the CPS online from Niche. It's incredibly intricate, illogical, and temperamental. You could write 50 pages explaining to a user what to click in what order to make it work. It was almost unheard of that when you finally hit the 'send' button TWIF wouldn't throw at least one obscure error back at you. TVP had an individual called the TWIF Tac-ad (tactical advisor) who was available during office hours. The TWIF Tac-ad was a dedicated person who had been trained in all the thousands of errors the TWIF system could produce and could help you resolve some of them.

Unfortunately, the TWIF Tac-ad was not available 24-7. So, if it was late at night and you were trying to send a remand file (a file you have to send if you want to remand someone in custody between their arrest and trial instead of bailing them or releasing them under investigation) before the PACE clock runs out, you would have to find and fix any errors yourself. Hours of wasted time and stress, all because of poor IT.

Then, in CID, I really started to notice the issue of police items that we frequently needed, and never had enough of. Evidence bags was a great example of this. There were different types and sizes of evidence bags that you used for different things – and if you were lucky, you would find an evidence bag in the drawer where it was supposed to be found. That was only if you were lucky, though. More often you would have to search the whole station, just to find something as simple as an evidence bag. Things were regularly missing from the car when you were out on patrol, too. You'd either have to improvise or ask a colleague to drop off the item you needed, wasting their time as well as yours.

I remember one particular moment where a rape had been reported and the uniform officers responding to the initial incident had no early evidence kit (EEK). An EEK contains equipment that allows an investigator to collect forensic evidence as soon as possible – obviously an important element of a rape investigation. ICR had none; other uniform officers came to the CID office to ask if we had one. We did not either. It took about half an hour to find an EEK somewhere in the station, after which it still had to be taken to the scene. After that, I kept one in my locker for emergencies. I could not bear the thought of being deployed to a rape and not having the required items to hand. Firstly, the whole point is to get the evidence rapidly – if you have to wait for a kit, crucial time could have passed. But more importantly, how would that affect the victim? What would they think? Could the victim still have faith in the professionalism of the police and our investigation? Ideally, the victim should not go to the loo, wash, or change before using the EEK; can you imagine being sexually assaulted and then being asked not to wash for half an hour while the police fumbled around looking for equipment?

After this incident I tried to order new stock for the office to make sure we had everything we needed. But it was incredibly difficult. In a truly baffling move, people kept denying that we were short on stock too – despite the blatant evidence all around. Other times I was told various reasons why I couldn't place an order: 'the order goes through automatically', 'oh, you don't have the authority to order items' (I have no idea if they were right, it was never explained who did have the authority to order items), 'oh, it's been ordered and will be there soon'. Even when I was told that, somehow we never seemed to receive those orders, and in the meantime officers would still be forced to go on an expedition to find something as simple as an evidence bag.

For reasons that escape me, nobody else seemed to be outraged, or even bothered, by this. Perhaps they had just got used to it by now. After all, I'd tried to do something about it and failed. And the level of bureaucracy involved in public sector procurement probably had a lot to do with the issues we faced. But to me, it was simply appalling.

These silly issues added so much extra stress, frustration (and sometimes embarrassment) to our lives. And they seemed to me easily resolvable.

CHAPTER 22

IIOC

A definite moment that stuck with me while at CID involved two IIOC cases – that's indecent images of children. The cases had been sent to us from the NCA, after two videos were flagged by TikTok and YouTube. Each was assigned to me and a colleague who we'll call Rob. Rob had been in CID for a few years, been an officer for a lot longer, and knew a lot. I liked him.

It may surprise you to know that the casefiles didn't include the videos themselves, just a description. As this was my only IIOC case I was involved in, I was never quite sure if this was standard procedure or not – but I suspect that it was. After all, if a video or image is graphic and upsetting, you may expose officers to unnecessary trauma by showing them the content. It's also likely that you'd need specialist training to be able to accurately identify what offences a particular image constitutes. It was odd reviewing the case with just a description of the videos, though.

I read the files braced for the worst – but found myself somewhat surprised by each case. One video contained an eight-year-old child filming themselves pulling their trousers down; the other was an eight-year-old child who had also uploaded a video of their private parts. The videos were evidently made by the children, but it was unclear whether an adult had instructed them to make these videos. So the first job for Rob and I was to carry out a safeguarding visit at the home address of each child. The aim of the visits was to speak to each child and get their side of the story, talk to the parents and ascertain what they knew, and to look for any signs of exploitation that might indicate we needed to take more action. On the drive over, I thought over and over again about how best to manage the visits. What would I say to the child, and to the parents, and so on. This was an odd case – it looked like some harmless videos made by children, but if it was something more than that it would be a serious case – and an opportunity to keep two children safe. I didn't want to miss anything.

We arrived at the first house.

"I'll take the lead on this one," Rob said, knocking on the door. I was happy to observe for this first one.

A man in his mid-40s opened the door.

"Hello, my name is Rob. I am a Detective. Can we come in for a moment to talk?" Rob said.

The man looked at our badges and ushered us in. We entered into the living room, and Rob got straight to the point.

"We're here because your son, Simon, has uploaded a naked video of himself on TikTok."

The man stared at us for a moment.

"TikTok…?" he asked.

"Yes, it's a social media platform," Rob replied. "Is your son, home?"

"Yes, he's upstairs." The man replied. To be honest, he struck me as pretty apathetic about the whole thing.

"Could you get him please?" Rob asked.

Simon came into the room holding his iPad. Rob sat him down on the sofa and asked him about the video. The boy thought for a moment.

"Oh yes, that video. No idea how it got posted to TikTok. Wasn't me."

I remember thinking to myself that children – or at least, poor Simon – aren't the best liars. It was plain as day that he knew exactly how the video had got online. His tone was painfully artificial, and his eyes were locked on the ceiling while he was talking to us.

Rob asked Simon a few more questions about the circumstances of the video and whether someone else was involved:

"Did someone else tell you to make that video?"

"Are you sure? I'm a police officer, it's OK to tell me the truth."

"Why did you make the video?"

"Why did you post it online?"

"Have you uploaded any other videos like that?"

Simon's answers left us satisfied there was no exploitation happening. He told us that nobody else was involved, and we believed him. He confirmed it was the only video, and that he hadn't really had anything in mind when he made it – and he wouldn't be doing it again.

That was a relief, of course. But that didn't mean our work was over. While Rob had been talking, I had been checking out the room. Part of the safeguarding work we had to do was making an informal assessment of the house. We were basically looking for any alarm bells that something was amiss and that the child in question might be at risk. Thankfully, Simon's house was very normal. He himself was dressed in clean clothes, seemed well-fed, and his house seemed in good condition.

Once we'd finished speaking to Simon, Rob talked to the father about letting his son use the iPad without supervision. As he had been at the front door, the father didn't seem terribly bothered about the whole incident but agreed to monitor his son's iPad use more closely. We also wrote a record visible to the MASH (multi-agency safeguarding hub) once we got back to the station.

MASHs are local arrangements that bring together as many different organisations involved in safeguarding as possible, so we can share information and ideally make the best decision for vulnerable people. So we filled out a 'child protection' form (if you remember the adult protection form we did for the man who told us he was in Hell's Angels, that also got submitted to the MASH). The child protection form then triggers a process where the MASH would decide whether to take further action or not.

A ten-minute drive later and we were at the next house – and it was my turn to take the lead. I'd called the landline earlier to see if they were at home, told them who I was, and that I needed to speak to them about their son. The father was alarmed on the phone.

"Why? What has happened? Has he done something? I don't understand," he blurted out.

I understood the confusion and upset, but told him I thought it was best to postpone the conversation for five minutes so we could have it face to face.

I rang the doorbell; a man and a woman led us into the living room. When I entered the living room I saw a boy sitting in the corner of the sofa. He looked as though he'd really rather the sofa swallowed him whole than have to talk to us. His discomfort was palpable. As soon as he saw me he pushed even deeper into the sofa, trying to cover his face with his arm.

"Haru, sit up straight and listen to the policewoman," his mother said sternly. Haru slowly appeared from the creases of the sofa and looked up scared.

I got straight to the point; I didn't want to draw out the suspense for the family any longer than I had to. I also felt quite sorry for poor Haru, suddenly having two intimidating police officers in his house to talk to him without knowing what it was about. I explained that there was a YouTube video in which Haru is seen to pull down his trousers and run around naked in the kitchen of the house.

While I was explaining all this, Haru's eyes became as large as tennis balls.

"It was Arthur's idea!" he shouted out as soon as I'd finished.

"Who is Arthur?" I asked.

His mother confirmed that Arthur was a school friend of Haru's, who was also eight years old. I asked the same follow up questions that we'd asked Simon, and was satisfied this was just done by two young boys as a joke and that there was no exploitation. To my relief (and unlike Simon's father), Haru's parents took the matter very seriously.

"Right! No iPad for a week, young man!" his father said sternly. Haru burst into tears. We still gave his parents some advice about supervision and technology; they assured us Haru would be much more tightly supervised from now on while using any electronic device. While we were talking, I was also looking around the house, making my informal assessment of the place and of the child. As with Simon's house, thankfully, there was nothing that rang any alarm bells. We said our thanks and goodbye.

Once out of earshot, Rob sniggered.

"He was very quick to throw his friend Arthur under the bus. You should have told him 'snitches get stitches'!"

As with the previous case, we submitted a report to the MASH, and as far as I know no further action was taken.

A final note on this story: the case files mentioned two eight-year old boys, but one of the boys Rob and I spoke to was ten years old. That's because it had taken two years for the case to land on our desks.

I'm not quite sure where the delay came from, but it could have been a number of places. There's a good chance that it took the review teams at YouTube and TikTok that long to get round to reviewing the content and flagging it as IIOC. After all, even with the AI-powered tools at their disposal, review teams are generally just groups of humans spending all their day watching horrendous content online to work out if it breaches their guidelines or shows criminal activity that needs to be passed to the police. These teams are usually far too small for the task they've been given, and I can only imagine the levels of burnout and absenteeism you get when your job is to watch awful stuff all day long. It's also possible that the case got lost with the NCA for a while – they're subject to the same bureaucracies and pressures that the rest of the police is.

Whatever the cause of the delay, in this particular instance I'm glad that, since there was no evidence of any exploitation, the delay didn't affect anyone's wellbeing. But if there had been exploitation or sexual abuse actually going on behind those videos, it would have essentially been prolonged by two years. Unfortunately, these types of delays weren't unusual in my experience of police work.

CHAPTER 23

TOOTHLESS TIGER

At one point in CID, I worked on a firearm possession case. The suspect in the case was a juvenile and lived in a care home, and was also heavily involved in drug dealing. After he was interviewed, our team sent a remand file to the CPS to keep him in custody for his own protection. This was rejected, as most remand applications for juveniles are – CPS don't want to keep juveniles on remand (in prison until their trial) unless it's absolutely necessary. It's partially a prison crowding thing, partially about the well-documented negative impacts of being in prison (especially on juveniles). So, instead, the suspect was put on pre-charge bail. One of the conditions of his bail was that he had to be at the care home between 9pm and 7am each day. Because investigations take an excruciatingly long time to complete, the juvenile was on bail for months until the point of charge by the CPS.

Throughout this period, the juvenile suspect breached his bail conditions almost daily. He would leave the care home late at night and not return until early in the morning. The staff at the care home contacted me at least once a week – usually more to make me aware of the breaches, wondering what I was going to do about it. I had to explain to them that all I could do at the moment was gather evidence of the breaches, but that we wouldn't be taking other action.

If that sounds strange to you, it definitely felt strange to me. But it was standard procedure – and if I was to arrest the suspect for breaching his bail conditions, I would likely have got in trouble with the custody sergeant. And it was all because the suspect was on pre-charge bail, often referred to as police bail by the public, or as the toothless tiger by the police.

Pre-charge bail is essentially used when there is not enough evidence after an interview to charge someone with an offence and there are further lines of enquiry to complete. In that situation, the police can either release a person under investigation (RUI), which means the investigation continues while the suspect is released from police custody, or release them on pre-charge bail. Pre-charge bail allows the police to set certain conditions that the suspect must abide by, such as reporting to a police station on a regular basis or not visiting certain locations. It's meant to control the risks the suspect poses to specific victims or society at large while the investigation is ongoing.

The problem is that pre-charge bail is not really enforceable. Although there is legislation that allows you to arrest a person for breaching their pre-charge bail conditions, that breach does not necessarily constitute an offence – so you wouldn't be able to charge them. Plus, under PACE, even though you can keep someone in custody for 24 hours without charge, once you've ascertained that you've not got any grounds to keep them in custody any more – for instance because they've not committed an offence and you can't charge them – you're supposed to let them go. That means that if you were to arrest someone for breaching pre-charge bail, it's likely you'd have to let them go almost immediately.

Because of this policing quirk, almost no arrests are made for breaches of pre-charge bail and officers were actively discouraged from doing so in practice by everyone from custody sergeants to station commanders. That's why police bail was referred to across Thames Valley Police as the toothless tiger. The only times I ever saw people making an arrest for breach of pre-charge bail was in serious DA cases where the suspect was likely to continue their abuse and put the victim in serious danger. You could also hope to find something else, which was enforceable, that you could arrest your suspect for – a separate offence such as witness intimidation for example. But even if you arrest for a new offence and can hold the suspect for 24h under PACE, the chances are the suspect will again be released with pre-charge bail conditions.

To return to our juvenile firearms offences suspect, I came to dread the weekly calls from the care home. Every conversation went the same way, and ended with us – the police – doing nothing. I had never expected that as a police officer I would feel so powerless so often. I started requesting video footage of the times he arrived at the care home past his curfew of 9pm and adding them to the casefile; there is a specific form you can attach to a casefile which details bail breaches and would, in theory, be taken into consideration during the court case. However, I've never seen evidence it was. The staff at the care home were unwilling to provide any statement to say they'd witnessed him breaching his bail conditions because they, understandably, did not want to damage their relationship with the suspect. It was a very frustrating few months.

Finally, the suspect was charged, and his bail conditions were changed from pre-charge to post-charge bail (also known as court bail). Breach of post-charge bail is enforceable, meaning a person can be arrested and remanded if they breach this type of bail. Once our suspect was given court bail he stopped breaching for a while, as he knew these bail conditions were enforceable. However, a few weeks later he did breach bail and was arrested and remanded in custody until he could be put before the court. I cannot remember the exact sentence he received in the end, but it may have been a youth caution – basically, a warning.

This case left me wondering: how can pre-charge bail ever protect victims? My conclusion was that it can't. Most experienced offenders know very well that there are no consequences to breaching police bail; I once stood at the desk with a regular burglary/robbery suspect.

As he was given his bail conditions he simply laughed and said:

"Nah, I'm not doing your conditions. Just letting you know now."

Part of me got his point. Why would anyone abide by a rule which is unenforceable and limits their freedom?

That particular incident was also memorable for a more amusing reason. The suspect was a frequent flyer with us, but I remember this time he'd given a particular type of 'no comment' interview: he stayed completely silent, with his eyes closed, as an extra 'fuck you' to us. As a consequence, I was leaving long pauses between questions – best practice is to give the suspect sufficient time to reply if they want to. And all of a sudden, his patience wore out.

"FUCKING GET ON WITH IT! I AM FUCKING CLUCKING!" he yelled.

For the uninitiated, clucking refers to being in withdrawal, often particularly from heroin. Supposedly it's because you shiver and have goose bumps – but don't quote me on that. Poor chap. Ironically, if he'd bothered to say 'no comment' instead of staying silent we would have been done faster and his suffering might have been alleviated sooner. But I digress.

You might wonder why the police even bother using the toothless tiger? There are a few reasons. As you know by now, police work is largely about covering your ass. Imposing pre-charge bail conditions is a tick in the box to show that the police is taking action to safeguard a victim (even though they are usually no safer). If the police were to release a suspect on RUI and they commit a serious further offence, the police will likely be criticised. Why didn't you impose bail to deter the suspect from committing further offences? If pre-charge bail is imposed on a suspect, the police can claim this was a safeguarding measure they took.

The next reason to impose pre-charge bail is that it does sometimes work on relatively cooperative and newbie suspects who don't know these bail conditions are not enforceable. If the suspects feel sufficiently intimidated by the process of being arrested and having pre-charge bail conditions imposed, they will stick to the conditions. But do you really need an elaborate system of pre-charge bail to essentially just bluff? I don't think you do. If someone is going to be cowed into accepting the terms of pre-charge bail, they are likely going to agree to your conditions whatever you call them.

Finally, as I said, in some DA cases officers did arrest for a breach of pre-charge bail. While they were usually not able to hold the suspect for long, it did serve to build trust with the victim, and (if the breach was because the suspect was harassing the victim) interrupt a potentially dangerous, or fatal, chain of events for the victim. It also sent a strong and clear message to the suspect that there would be consequences to their actions. But we didn't do this for every DA case, or every time, and it didn't always work – some offenders continued to breach bail until we could remand them in custody.

The lack of action after a breach is one of the biggest reasons that I think pre-charge bail damages the trust in the police. Consider if a DA victim summons up the courage to report an abusive partner to the police. Their hope is that the partner is locked up and kept away from them for good – so the subsequent release is usually very scary. The police then calm the victim down by saying the suspect has bail with conditions, and the victim is urged to report any breaches of these conditions as soon as they can. This of course makes the victim feel safer – but when the conditions are breached and the victim calls the police to report… frequently, nothing happens.

In that situation, the victim understandably feels let down and unsupported by the police. Bearing in mind how frightened and vulnerable some of the victims can feel, that breakdown in trust can lead the victim to withdraw their prior statement and instil a strong reluctance to call the police again in the future. The victim might even go back to managing their own safety, which is likely to lead to more violence and possibly deaths.

CHAPTER 24

THE POLICE AGENDA

The topic of covering your ass has come up quite a bit so far; at CID it was just as much a factor as at any other department. Covering your ass formed part of what's known in police circles as 'the police agenda'. At Sully, it was explained to us that in any given case, there are generally two agendas at play: the police agenda, and the victim agenda.

Simply put, the victim often has different priorities and wants to the police. The police are interested in making sure they have completed all their procedures correctly and got all the evidence they need. The victim has their own agenda which can include things like feeling safe, recovering stolen property or getting financial compensation. The victim certainly isn't interested in police paperwork.

At Sully, we were taught to prioritise the victim's agenda before the police's (remember, 'victim-first' is the watchword of any police strategy). In practice, however, I more often saw us tackle the police agenda first, with the victim's agenda coming a distant second or sometimes being ignored entirely. I can understand and rationalise some of this when I think about the pressure officers are under, the events they see and witness every day, and the physical and mental strain of the job. But by the time I got to CID, this prioritising of the police agenda was really starting to grate on me. Especially since the number one thing on the police agenda was covering your ass.

I always expected that the guiding principle in my job as a police officer would be something like 'doing the right thing' or 'helping people'. I suppose those are subjective concepts, but they would have been better than the one thing that seemed to be on everyone's mind: making sure nobody could criticise you. All the box-ticking, form-filling, and so on left a bitter taste in my mouth, because we always seemed to be doing it for the sake of it – or rather, so that we wouldn't get in trouble for not doing it. Were we really trying to help people or were we just trying not to get fired?

The Slough jobs that I encountered in CID were where I felt this the most. One such example was the time when a third party had reported that a local well-known criminal had been punched in the face, likely causing injuries consistent with GBH. Because GBHs fall within CID's remit, the event was recorded as a crime and allocated to my team. Two officers from the team went to see the local criminal – let's call him Steve – at his home address. They knocked on the window, and Steve opened his window to talk to them. The officers explained why they were there – they'd had a report Steve had been assaulted, and they wanted to check on him.

"Fuck off!" Steve shouted aggressively.

Now, to me, this would have been case closed. In the first place, it was unclear whether the assault actually happened. And in the second, the victim clearly wanted nothing to do with us. But I was wrong. When my colleague told sergeant Fara what had happened – and that Steve had told them to fuck off – she thought for a moment.

"Hmm… let's try again tomorrow."

I was incredulous. It seemed outrageous that we would go back to this case when the victim had told us to fuck off. But it does not look good to close a GBH investigation like that. We needed to show on paper that we'd tried harder to engage with the victim and solve the crime before we could close the case. Even though everyone knew it was pointless. Where was the room for us to use our personal judgement? Was it likely, at all, that Steve would appear at his front door tomorrow with a sunny disposition and a willingness to talk to the police? Hardly.

Sometimes these kinds of cases culminated in what is called a memorandum of understanding (MOU). An MOU is an official document which advises the person to cooperate with police for their own wellbeing, which we could serve to any victim of crime who was refusing to cooperate. We had to ask the victim to sign the MOU to prove that they understood what we were saying – but regardless of whether they did or didn't sign, the MOU added another layer of ass-covering for us.

An even thornier case that I remember involved a well-known criminal who had come out of prison to find that his girlfriend had cheated on him with a rival criminal. The OIC on the case told me that we had intel on our systems that suggested this was true (don't ask me how we knew that, or why – I have no idea!). When the criminal confronted his girlfriend about it, the girlfriend told him she hadn't cheated but that in fact she was raped. The boyfriend went nuts and called the police, demanding that we investigate.

Of course, we did start investigating – but the girlfriend laid low and avoided police at all costs. She didn't answer the door, she didn't answer phone calls. Based on the intel we had, it seemed to us that she wanted the case to go away because it was all a lie to cover up her infidelity. Even if the rape did happen, the victim clearly did not want any police involvement. Meanwhile we were spending hours investigating. Obtaining and analysing CCTV footage, conducting house-to-house enquiries, and so on, because we had to go through the motions for the record. All the while, we all felt certain that this case would inevitably be filed (meaning that we'd be taking no further action, and not charging anyone) as there was zero evidence and the victim had gone off the radar. Filing this case was particularly difficult though because TVP was desperately trying to increase its charge and conviction rates for serious sexual offences. Of course, in the end, it was filed – and rightly so. It was the only possible outcome.

As with the other case, it's not the processes and bureaucracy that I objected to, per se. It was that we had to do it even though everyone knew the case wasn't going anywhere. In our training at Sully, we were taught to be inquisitive, to challenge things, and to think critically. All of those instincts would lead us to drop both of these cases, and instead focus on getting faster results in other cases. But we were up against a rigid bureaucracy that insisted we go through every step, for every case, regardless of the circumstances. It was frustrating, to say the least.

Even when it was clear that a crime had been committed and we had a victim that needed help, the principle of ass-covering often worked against us. After CID, I did a spell in the domestic abuse unit (which we'll come to later in the book). DA cases often involve a thing called a MARAC meeting before which we were supposed to try everything we could to speak to victim. MARAC stands for multi-agency risk assessment conference, and is a meeting between a number of agencies designed to protect the victim of abuse and to deal with the perpetrator.

There was one victim in particular whose case I was the OIC for. A family member had contacted us about her, and as a result she had been spoken to several times by various agencies and had been given information about support. Though she maintained that nothing had happened and there was no problem, TVP had completed a risk assessment and safety plan with her about a week ago. However, that was saved as a separate log in the system – which meant that, according to procedure, we had to do the risk assessment and safety plan again with the victim before the MARAC meeting. It quickly became clear that the victim was dodging us – she didn't respond to our calls, or our texts, or to us knocking on the door. During the case I reviewed bodycam footage of her saying several times that she did not want to speak to police anymore, and repeating her assertion that nothing had happened.

I sympathised with the victim's wish to not speak to us; we'd effectively bombarded her with the same questions, assessments and safety plans for two weeks, and now we were coming back for a third time to get the same information and ask the same questions. It was becoming clear to me that the victim would certainly think twice about ever calling us for help if our approach continued like this. But, of course, our actions weren't about what was right for her – they were about what was right for us. The police agenda was coming first again. We needed to have enough evidence that we'd done our jobs right that if something went horribly wrong, we couldn't be blamed.

So, I went to her home address and knocked on the door. The door was on the high street next to an off-licence shop. When there was no answer, I asked the guy behind the counter in the off-licence. He said he knew the victim, but that she'd gone out earlier that day. He also told me that there was no point knocking on the door, because behind it was a long hallway and staircase up to the front door of the victim's flat – something I later confirmed watching the body worn video from attending officers at the flat. There was no way in hell that a knock on that door would be heard upstairs in their flat. I explained that to the sergeant and said it would be pointless to go back to knock on the door.

"I understand," he said, "but go anyway because than we can say we tried."

I went back twice to the address to go through the motions of knocking, knowing it was entirely pointless. I hated it. In many ways, the bureaucracy and procedures we had to go through were designed to remove individual judgement from cases – often because an error of judgement had caused something to go wrong. But my experience was that using no personal judgement, ever, was just as damaging as the risk of someone's faulty judgement causing problems. The whole reason police officers were encouraged to use their brains was that so many cases that had fallen apart (or something had gone horribly wrong) because officers were simply going through the motions and they were not professionally curious. If they were using their heads, perhaps those errors wouldn't have happened.

CHAPTER 25

TRAFFIC

One of the drawbacks of being in the investigative units, for a rookie like me, was that I was struggling to tick off the more operational elements needed in my policing portfolio. The portfolio is a part of your probation, and is essentially your evidence that you've done enough of the different elements of policing needed to become a full-fledged officer. In my case, I needed more arrests and searches for my portfolio – and I also needed to give out a ticket and search a car. To help me with those last two, about five or six months into my time in CID, Fara decided to send me on a two-day attachment with the road traffic unit.

I was quite excited to see how the road traffic unit worked, and learn more about roads policing. It's such a niche area of policing, with so many laws and rules unique to it, that it's very hard for someone not in the unit to wrap their head around. Even experienced officers who weren't in the road traffic unit were unfamiliar with half of what went on. But I was also nervous about putting on a uniform again and facing the unknown. Would there be violence? Knives? Car crashes?

For my time on the traffic unit I was crewed with a young friendly guy who we'll call Chung. Chung had a few years of experience in traffic. There were no newbies in the unit; because traffic policing is a specialist unit, you can only apply to join after finishing your probation – meaning that everyone knows what they're doing. Even from my brief glimpse, I could see that it was a smaller unit where everyone seemed closer than they did in other units, which looked like a pretty sweet deal. We had a good time chatting in the car, where I picked his brains on some of the intricacies of traffic policing. Then we got our first call. There had been an accident on the motorway – thankfully just some material damage, and no injuries. However, the debate between the two drivers as to who was at fault got a bit heated, to the point that one of them decided to call the police and walk away from the situation.

That was my first blue light run on a motorway; it was scarily fast. I remember thinking at the time that I might never get used to this kind of speed – though Chung, who was the one doing the actual driving, looked reasonably relaxed. Perhaps it's more relaxing to drive at 110mph when you're the one in control of the wheel.

By the time we arrived at the scene, the situation already seemed to have diffused somewhat. We met the driver who had called us. We stood on the hard shoulder as he tried hard to convince us that he was in the right, justify his actions, and explain why he called us. Behind the hard shoulder, in the bushes and grass, hid a younger man – the other driver. He seemed a bit taken aback by what was going on. We reassured him that we'd sort everything out, and facilitated the exchange of details between the two drivers.

Next, we ran them through the system to check whether either they or the vehicles had any outstanding warrants, expired MOTs, or similar – or rather, I tried to. To do vehicle and person checks we used an app called Pronto, which you may remember I'd already done a training module on while waiting for some cases to come my way at the start of CID. Unfortunately, investigation teams rarely used Pronto, and my training module obviously hadn't sunk in because I had almost no idea how to use it. Chung, thank god, was very helpful, and helped me get through what felt like 25 steps in the app to do the check.

I got through the check – and the app crashed. Chung lent me his phone so I could try again.

The check ran successfully this time, but now I had no idea where and how to read the results the app was showing me. Unfortunately, a mix of complex procedures, sensitive data, and terrible design meant that very few police systems were intuitive to use – hence the raft of training courses.

"It says 'no insurance found'" I said to Chung.

"No, ignore that part," he said, "it doesn't work. You need to search that on another system."

I couldn't help but think that if I had been on my own, I would have failed miserably to do even the most basic check of the vehicle.

The check revealed no outstanding issues, so we finished up with the drivers and were soon back on the road again.

"Let's try and get you a ticket!" Chung said, a happy expression on his face.

We drove into Slough and parked up on a road.

"This road is usually where people speed," said Chung. We waited around for little while but on this occasion, it seemed, the people of Slough had decided to be careful around here. We were on our way to another location to look for speeders when Chung spotted the driver of a white van.

"No seat belt!" he said with some excitement. We happened to be next to the driver while he was waiting at a traffic light, so I rolled down my window and asked the driver to pull over.

"How did you see that?" I asked as the van driver pulled over. "We were so far away from that van!"

"You get good at spotting these things," he answered triumphantly.

We stopped behind the driver of the white van. He was a man in his 20s, who was delivering parcels.

"I really apologise," he said straightaway.

"We're gonna have to give you a ticket," I said.

"Please," he said, looking rather desperate, "is it possible to get a warning?"

I hesitated. Could I just give him a warning? I was about to agree but Chung was quicker.

"I'm afraid not," he said, handing me the ticket booklet.

The ticket was (of course) a lengthy form and I had to ask Chung at several stages what certain parts meant or what to fill in. If the driver had been less compliant, I thought to myself, I'd never have been able to fill this form in and this would have been hugely stressful. The driver, however, remained polite and calm.

I felt bad about giving him a ticket. Although it's against the law to drive without a seat belt, I could totally imagine as a parcel deliverer that it's something you could forget to do or decide not to do because it's only a one-minute drive to the next drop-off point. I felt bad that this guy had gotten a ticket essentially for me to tick a box in my portfolio.

By the end of that first shift, I felt completely destroyed. I'm reasonably sure that I didn't let Chung see it, but through the entire shift I could feel anxiety vibrating through my body. I'd never been an anxious person by nature, but getting back into the uniform for my day with the traffic unit put me into fight or flight mode for eight hours solid. I just couldn't relax. At all. Looking back, this was probably the first major red flag that my work in the police was starting to tear me apart.

I knew that anxiety could wear your mind down, but this was the first time I'd experienced the accompanying physical fatigue that anxiety causes, too. I crawled home, and didn't have the energy to do anything more than lie in bed and watch some easy TV. Neither my brain nor my body could handle anything more than that. The thought of doing any hobbies, or going out to see friends, felt like a distant dream – far too much stimulation for my cortisol-flooded brain. I had no idea how I was going to make it through my second day with the road traffic unit.

Nevertheless, day two arrived and we were back out on the roads, trying to catch someone speeding. Today we tried the foot of a hill in a 30mph zone, Chung ready with his speed gun. Soon, a small Ford came down the hill going at 40mph. Chung flagged the car down and I explained to the driver that we would give her a speeding ticket. The driver was a woman in her 40s who told us she was on the way to school to pick up her kids. Unfortunately for her, she couldn't leave before I finished writing yet another lengthy ticket form. At the end of the form I also had to recite certain predefined wording to the woman – a bit like the caution you give when arresting someone, though obviously the woman was not under arrest. She was visibly annoyed by the whole situation, but stayed polite, for which I was thankful.

I felt pretty similarly about fining this woman as I had for fining the parcel driver the day before. It was like we weren't doing this to keep people safe, but for my own personal gain instead. Of course, speeding can be very dangerous indeed – but I was looking at her driving as she came down the hill, and it didn't look dangerous to me. I personally wanted to let her off with a warning and accept the empty tick box. This and the driver the day before felt like the kinds of situations where someone might (legitimately) say 'don't you have something better to do? Like catching real criminals?'

At the very least, I thought, we could have waited for a Porsche or Range Rover to give tickets to, knowing they probably had some money to spare. Instead, I gave the tickets to a hard-working delivery driver, who probably doesn't have an abundance of cash, and a mother on the school run driving a little Ford hatchback. It couldn't be worth it.

I told Chung how I felt, and he laughed.

"I used to feel like that when I started out," he said, "but not anymore. You get used to it. After all, it's that person's mistake. Not mine."

He was right, of course, but at the time I thought: 'wow, Chung is so jaded!' I wondered if perhaps that was something you needed to be, to survive in this job. After all, Jay had been very jaded, and he was doing fine.

After we'd eaten our lunch and completed our paperwork at the station, we went back on patrol, to listen to the near-constant ping of number plates being flagged by our ANPR system. Roads policing cars all have an Automatic Numberplate Recognition (ANPR) system which is linked to the police database. It's a great idea – if a car drives past that's marked as wanted on police systems, or is recorded as stolen, or as being driven without insurance, you can pick them up. However, in classic TVP style, the system didn't quite live up to expectations. The records were often out of date, and though it still gave you an opportunity to stop a vehicle and investigate further if you felt it was needed, it was easy to get blind to all the pings. Chung ignored most of them.

"Aren't we supposed to stop these cars?" I asked him eventually.

"No, these pop ups aren't reliable," he said. "I'll tell you when we find one which is." To this day, I have no idea how he would know – perhaps, I wondered, he was simply so familiar with the cars in the area that he could recognise numberplates of interest on sight.

Once again, I had no clue how the ANPR system worked, and without Chung I wouldn't have been able to use it at all. These were the kinds of things you could not read up on in books either. You just had to find out by trial and error, or rely on colleagues to teach you.

A little later we got a ping on the dashboard telling us that a car that just passed on the opposite side of the road had no insurance. This one must have been reliable, because Chung turned around swiftly and switched on the blue lights. Once the car had pulled over, Chung and I walked up to the window

The window rolled down to reveal a young man, and a strong smell of cannabis that hit me as I was telling him we'd stopped him for a check.

"Please step out of the vehicle," Chung said. I proceeded to tell the guy he was being detained for a search.

The man was cooperative; you could see on his face that he knew he'd been caught and there wasn't going to be any getting out of it. I searched the vehicle and confiscated his grinder and a small bag of cannabis – sorry, I mean his small bag of green herbal matter. I arrested him for drug driving (yay, another arrest to put on my portfolio), and continued to search the car. It was very messy with clothes, food, litter, and other items scattered around it. There was nothing else amiss, however.

Search completed, I got back into the police car, where the young man was sitting in the back. We were about to head to the station when he suddenly shouted:

"Oh, wait! My son's school uniform. It's in the boot. His mum is going to kill me if I don't have it."

I went back to the car and started digging through the mess in the booth.

"What colour is it?" I asked him – the state of the boot meant that it was hard to spot anything. Finally, I found it and we headed to the station.

The man was very tall, and wore a Trapstar tracksuit and hoodie. He was friendly with us and we chit-chatted on the way to the station. Although I questioned his decision making, I instantly liked him. For once, the small talk actually felt natural; we found out we had the same favourite stand-up comedian. It did occur to me at a few points in my career that perhaps I was too soft-hearted to be a police officer!

When we arrived at the station, we were sent to the custody HCP (healthcare practitioner) to take a blood sample. We needed that to prove that the man had indeed driven under the influence of cannabis. Interestingly, neither a breathalyser or a roadside drug test counts as an 'evidential test' – meaning it's not reliable enough to be used in evidence. It is grounds enough for the police to bring you to the station though, where they can do an evidential breath test for alcohol or a blood test for drugs which is accurate enough to be used as evidence.

"I hate needles" the guy said.

Sure enough, and as soon as we went into the nurse's room, he turned into a small child.

"I can't look!" he panicked with his face in a grimace and his eyes closed. As the needle went in he started screaming – though to his credit he did hold his arm in place. Chung and I couldn't help but giggle to ourselves a little as this tough guy with his Trapstar tracksuit squirmed and squealed his way through a simple blood test. The juxtaposition was just too obvious.

After the sample had been taken and the man had calmed down, he was released.

"Maybe there wasn't enough blood in the sample," Chung said to him. "Maybe you'll get lucky and the sample will be declared void for that reason."

Does that sound weird to you, a police officer saying that to a suspect? Stuff like that happened more often than you'd think. Building rapport, after all, doesn't stop when you get to the station. There was every chance that we'd see this young man again – so it was important that he not think of us as the enemy any more than we could help. Plus, as I said, sometimes you just get on with a suspect. Obviously, neither of us was hoping that the course of justice would be thwarted by a bad blood test – but it cost us nothing to say, and it helped us stay on his good side.

As we drove back to the station, Chung said to me:

"You know, you'd make a great uniform officer. You know how to talk to people. That's so important."

In that moment, the compliment meant more to me than I could say. As I lay at home later, trying to rest my body and mind after another crushing day of high-alert stress levels, those words went round my head like a firefly, glowing in the gathering dark.

CHAPTER 26

GBH

My first charge in CID came after a few months. It was a fairly straightforward charge for GBH: a man in his 20s had punched another man in his 20s on a night out. The incident was caught on CCTV and witnessed by security staff; the suspect was arrested at the scene and was compliant. He had no previous criminal record or run ins with police. The victim was taken to hospital with severe swelling to his eye and cheek. All in all, pretty standard fare when policing the night-time economy. I was OIC, so I went to interview the suspect with a colleague.

The interview was very surprising. The suspect refused his right to a solicitor and gave a full account of the incident, in which he admitted the offence without excuses or defences.

"Yeah, it was a fight over nothing really," he said. "The other guy shoved his way past me, which I didn't like, and when I confronted him about it he didn't bother apologising. He just shrugged the whole thing off. So, I got angry and security chucked me out of the club."

"What happened next?" I asked.

"Well, I was even angrier now, 'cos he'd ruined my night out. So I hung around, and as soon as I saw him come out of the club I punched him in his face. I know I shouldn't have done it. I guess I was just too angry to care."

My colleague and I both had mixed feelings about this confession. On the one hand, his honesty was refreshing, and we were impressed that he had the integrity to take responsibility for his actions. But on the other hand, we were struck by the naivety of admitting such a serious offence without first consulting a solicitor. Even though my colleague and I impressed upon him from the start that this was a serious offence, it was clear that the gravity of the situation hadn't dawned on him.

The penny dropped when I showed him the injury photos taken by my colleagues at the hospital. They weren't nice to look at, showing as they did the severe swelling to the victim's face that was the result of the assault. As soon as he saw the pictures, the man winced, turned his head away, and covered his face with his hands. I thought he was going to cry – it's a pretty common reaction from suspects who haven't had much to do with the police, once they realise the trouble they're in.

"Oh my god," he quavered, sounding right on the verge of tears, "I am so sorry… I didn't know it was this bad."

As we finished the interview, it was plain from the suspect's face that he was panicking as the realisation that he was in deep shit sunk in. After the interview was finished, he asked us:

"Is there anything I can do to make this better? I want to apologise to the victim."

"No," replied my colleague, "you have to stay away from him. You'll likely be given bail conditions not to contact him."

Later on, I went to visit him in his custody cell to ask him about his current home address – I was planning on imposing bail conditions which required the suspect to live and sleep at a specific address. The suspect was still in a state of anxiety and worry, asking us what was going to happen and if he was going to go to prison. I have to say that I couldn't help feeling a little sorry for him. What he had done was completely unacceptable, of course. But he was the only suspect I'd dealt with so far that had been honest during his interview, and who had shown genuine remorse for a mistake he'd made. To me that was worth something.

Amazingly, during the investigation the suspect called me several times to ask questions about his bail conditions, court dates, probation appointments, and his legal representation. Even though I couldn't answer all his questions, I told him where he could find the answers and who he should contact. It was clear that he was struggling to understand the process (not surprising, since I worked for the police and was still trying to understand it myself). I suppose that I must have come across as fair and trustworthy for him to feel comfortable speaking to me, the officer leading the investigation in which he was the suspect.

As part of the investigation, I also took a victim statement about a week and a half after the assault. Luckily the injury to the victim's face had healed without permanent damage, and it seemed as though he had moved on from the incident.

Even though the investigation was very straightforward, it took a long time to process. When I eventually sent off the case files to the CPS, I got an answer back about two and a half weeks later. My suspect was formally charged with GBH.

"Congratulations," Fara said as I made tea in the kitchen. "Your first charge! Great result." The inspector approached me too.

"Congrats on your first charge," she said. "That must feel good".

I nodded, but in truth it didn't feel that good. There had been so many occasions up until now where bad people had gotten away with their crimes. This time, someone who had made a mistake – but was willing to take responsibility for it – was likely to get a serious sentence handed down to him.

At the plea hearing the suspect pleaded guilty. In case you're not familiar with how pleas work, the plea hearing is basically a chance for the suspect to say whether they agree with the charges brought against them. Any charges that you plead guilty to, essentially, won't go to trial, because you've already admitted your guilt. If you plead 'not guilty' to some or all of the charges against you, the case will go to trial.

Although guilty pleas can often be sentenced there and then, because of the severity of this offence sentencing had to take place in Crown court, rather than in the magistrates court. The sentence was passed down a few months later, and about eight or nine months after the original incident. The suspect was given a prison sentence of a little more than a year. I updated the victim, and he seemed surprised at the verdict. After all, he'd put the incident behind him months ago. Still, he thanked me for letting him know and for the work I put into the case. It felt good receiving appreciation and positive feedback from a victim at the conclusion of a case.

However, I still felt bad for the suspect. I definitely thought he should be punished, but a prison sentence of over a year seemed disproportionate.

Firstly, the guy had no previous convictions. Secondly, he had showed genuine remorse for his actions. Was the suspect really such a risk to the public that he should be locked up for over a year? Thirdly, the victim had made a full recovery and the incident hadn't had a long-lasting negative impact on his life. In contrast, the suspect's life was going to be forever stained by his criminal record on top of the prison sentence. It would surely affect his ability to get work in the future and other opportunities.

I thought about my first ever charge, the man who assaulted the NHS staff members and verbally abused me for half an hour. Despite the charge, he was still out on bail and was wreaking havoc at least once a week. The members of staff he terrorised were scared to go back to work for fear of another assault. It was only a matter of time before it happened again.

In short, I was coming to loathe the justice system. Its complexity and quirks seemed to be constantly leading to these bizarre circumstances where criminals that showed remorse and cooperated with the system were punished more harshly than those who worked hard to cause trouble and had no regard for the rule of law. I was able to partially console myself that as an investigator, my role was impartial. I wasn't trying to get specific individuals charged with offences, but to get to the truth of my cases. I was supposed to follow all lines of enquiry, whether they pointed to the suspect or away from them. At least I could say that I didn't set out to be a part of these unfair decisions. But I couldn't deny that my work played a part in those decisions, and that knowledge slowly, painfully, eroded my enthusiasm for my work.

CHAPTER 27

LIVE KIDNAP AND MAJOR CRIMES

If you've watched a police show, there's a good chance you'll be familiar with the term 'Major Crime Unit', 'Major Crimes', or something similar. And if you ever watched *Catching a Killer*, you'll have heard of the Thames Valley Police Major Crime Unit, or MCU for short. The MCU is a prestigious unit that deals with the big crimes such as murders. The MCU has three offices covering different areas of Thames Valley (TVP is the largest non-metropolitan police force in England and Wales, covering 2,218 square miles). The MCU works pretty much like you've seen on TV. If a crime falls under their remit, then they descend upon the local station and take direct control of whatever resources they need to run the investigation. You might remember them from my first day of CID, when I walked into a sea of unfamiliar people and lots of activity as there was a murder case in progress.

Pretty much everything about the MCU worked differently to regular policing. They had a different IT system (which presumably worked better than Niche), and different procedures to follow. As a rule, they were extremely detailed. Every thought and action was meticulously recorded. They were also extremely controlling. If you were under the command of the MCU there was little to no room for initiative; every action needed to be carried out very specifically on the orders of the SIO (Senior Investigating Officer) from the MCU.

Needless to say, though the MCU guys did a good job, the way things worked often led to frustrations and confusion for local officers. It's a strange feeling, being in charge of a case one minute and then the next losing all control of it to the MCU. It sometimes happened with suspicious death investigations. CID would be investigating, we started to think it might be a murder case, and the MCU would swoop in. Sometimes it would become apparent that it wasn't a murder, and they would drop the case back in our lap – but because the MCU uses a different system, we wouldn't be able to access any of their case files and would either have to wait for them to download their case files and send them to us, or essentially start again.

As well as murders, the MCU dealt with stranger rapes and live kidnaps – the 'gucci' jobs, to give you another bit of slang from the station. A 'live kidnap' essentially refers to a scenario where someone is currently kidnapped, and the police should act fast to get them back safely. I was once involved in a case deemed a 'live kidnap' that allowed me to see how the MCU works up close.

The case: a 16-year-old girl, who we'll call Aya, had recently moved to the UK as a refugee with her family. Aya's mother called the police one evening to say that she'd seen her daughter being picked up by an unknown black car outside the house in the evening and she'd not heard from her daughter since – about three hours before she called. She had no idea who had picked Aya up, and the only other information she gave us was that her daughter was a bit rebellious and had struggled with the transition of moving to the UK.

I was on an early shift, so shortly after 8am I was at their house speaking to Aya's mother and brother, with a colleague who we'll call Esme. The mother was plainly worried sick, and couldn't stop pacing around the living room. By now, Aya had been out all night and nobody had heard from her. The mother didn't speak English, but her son (Aya's older brother), spoke a little. The brother had reached out to two guys who he believed Aya was with. They were both teenagers from the same country as Aya and her family, so it was a reasonable supposition. While we were there, one of them replied to Aya's brother on Instagram and said that he was with Aya but that she wasn't coming home yet. Nothing more.

That might sound like a relatively innocuous message, but it came alongside a number of other red flags. Flag one: nobody knew where Aya was. Flag two: nobody had been able to speak to Aya herself to verify that she was going willingly with these people. And now, flag number three, one of the boys had messaged us to tell her she wasn't coming home. I was relaying all the information back to the CID office, and once enough pieces had fallen into place someone higher up the chain deemed the situation a live kidnap.

As soon as this label was applied, it wasn't long before the MCU arrived at the station and started commandeering our resources. An analyst was looking into the Instagram profile, while another team was conducting CCTV enquiries. I was ordered to stay with the family in case they needed to answer more questions, or in case Aya came home. The MCU kept calling with further questions for the family, most of which we asked via an interpreter. Any police officer can call an interpreter line during work, but it's not a great way to communicate so sometimes we try to work with an informal third party. Given the seriousness of the incident, though, we decided to switch from relying on Aya's brother for translation duties to using a professional interpreter.

Seeing interpreters on the TV or in movies never accurately conveys what a complex process it is. In the first place, the conversations all take twice – if not three times – as long just because you have another person in the mix. On top of that, the risk of miscommunication is very high due to the different ways of expressing thoughts and ideas in different languages. So there's often lots of going back over things to make sure that we've not misunderstood what is being said to us, or that the person being interviewed hasn't misunderstood us. But I digress.

Once the whirlwind of MCU establishing themselves had passed, I discovered that being part of an MCU investigation often feels weirdly still. Often you're only assigned one task, meaning that a lot of the time you are waiting for instructions, or simply waiting to do your specific job. As I said, the MCU wants complete control over every action and every detail of the case. Unless there are exceptional circumstances, you're not allowed to take initiative or be proactive without checking in with the person in charge first. So I spent much of the investigation sitting on the family's sofa in their living room with Esme.

It felt strange to be sat there while a young person was potentially in danger. Via the translator, I felt the need to explain to the family that we had a whole team on the case who were following up on all the information the family provided, lest the family think we weren't taking things seriously.

After another couple of hours, two more colleagues from CID came to the house and joined us. I wasn't entirely sure why.

"We want to ask the family some more questions," they said. Quite why they needed to come down instead of us asking the questions is beyond me. But that's how it is when the MCU is in charge of an investigation. They make the decisions, you carry them out – regardless of how much sense they make in the moment.

"Mark my words, she'll show up here in a moment," said Esme.

And, sure enough, after another hour or so – about 3pm – the doorbell suddenly rang. It was Aya.

"AYA!" Shouted her mother, relief and anger warring in her voice. And she started talking to her rapidly in their language. Aya's younger brother, who was about 11 years old and had spent most of the time up to now upstairs or milling about the house, came to the door to see the commotion. Even though I didn't speak the language, it was plain as day that he said something along the lines of:

"Ha! Aya the police are here for you," with a smirk on his face. Interestingly, the word 'police' sounds pretty similar in a lot of languages.

Aya was brusque and said almost nothing to anyone. Instead, she tried to quietly make her way upstairs.

"Aya," Esme and I said sternly, "we need to have a word."

Aya quietly came back down the stairs, radiating the carefully constructed sense of indifference that teenagers all over the world seem to develop. She spoke no English at all, so we used another interpreter (we'd hung up on our previous one, and when you call back you just get allocated the next available interpreter). Meanwhile, one of my colleagues had already informed the SIO.

Esme and I started interviewing Aya via the interpreter on the phone.

Aya told us she met an 18-year-old guy on Instagram who was from her home country. After chatting for a while they decided to meet to go for a drive. He picked her up in the car and they drove to London where they met a few of the guy's other friends. Aya told us that they were in the park all night having a good time, chatting.

"Did you take any alcohol, or drugs?" I asked her.

"I drank a little bit of rum," she admitted.

"Did anything happen that you did not like or that felt uncomfortable?" I asked.

"No," she replied.

I probed a little more around this topic. As a police officer, your training and experience lead you to consider the worst-case scenario in any incident. In this particular example – a young girl out drinking with a group of people she'd never met before – my instinct was to check whether she was sexually assaulted.

My probing, however, revealed that Aya had simply engaged in a bit of teenage rebellion. Taking off without saying where she was going, and a bit of experimenting with alcohol and a boy she fancied. She said that nothing happened and they just got to know each other; I believed her. Even so, I gave her my card and told her she could always give me a call if she wanted to speak about anything. With that, we finished the interview and hung up the phone to the interpreter.

Aya asked if she could go to bed. She'd been up all night and felt exhausted.

"Not yet. We first need to speak to the investigation team," Esme said. I called the MCU sergeant and relayed the information we'd got, expecting things to end here for the day. But I was wrong. The sergeant had prepared a list of further questions, which the two colleagues who arrived earlier asked Aya in minute detail.

During this exchange, I was informed that one of the guys who was with Aya last night was arrested. I imagined his arrest would come as a shock if everything Aya said was true. Meanwhile, my two colleagues had got a little more detail from Aya but her story remained the same. No crime, just a rebellious evening out with a boy. After about an hour of questioning, Aya was allowed to go to bed and rest. As were we – it was the end of our shift, so Esme and I went back to the station and headed home.

I was slightly incredulous at the way things had gone – mainly the level of scrutiny that the MCU had brought with them. It definitely felt like the police agenda had bulldozed all over the family we were supposed to be helping, and I couldn't help wonder how much we'd even helped at all. Of course, I was glad that Aya had returned home safely, and it was right to escalate the case to the MCU based on what we knew at the time. But all we'd done was question Aya to within an inch of her life. We didn't even find her – she came home by herself.

The next day I came into the office and saw Esme.

"I was a bit surprised at how much Aya was grilled yesterday," I remarked. "I thought we covered the important parts in our first chat with her. I think MCU were convinced that she was raped or sexually assaulted."

Esme grinned suddenly. "Poor kid. They went back to her house twice today to ask her exactly the same questions."

CHAPTER 28

MY FIRST DEAD BODY

Your first 'sudden death' (as they call it) is a relatively big thing in the police. Every officer knows that, sooner or later, they'll come across a dead body. For some recruits, it might be the first dead body they've ever seen. I saw lots of officers try to support their colleagues through that moment by sharing their own sudden death stories. At first it seems to be a way of showing that they understand what a new recruit is going through when they experience their first sudden death – but inevitably those conversations turn into a bit of a competition to see who has the most gruesome sudden death story. Badly decomposed bodies, bodies missing limbs – hang around a group of police officers long enough, and you'll hear stories about them all.

The police was not my first experience with dead bodies. In my family, I had been by the bedside of every one of my grandparents when they passed away. It was a family thing, it seemed, and I count myself lucky to have experienced it. None of my grandparents died suddenly, so we all had a chance to say goodbye and show them that they were surrounded by love as they passed. Don't get me wrong – they were all very sad experiences. But they also had an element of peace and closure that was enormously valuable.

Because of these experiences I had perhaps seen more dead bodies than many of my course mates at Sully. Certainly when the topic came up during training, I wasn't scared or worried about seeing a dead body. The only thing going through my head was wanting to make sure I could do my job right and be professional – partly for the family, and partly for the deceased person.

I definitely got the sense that my course mates were more worried about having to give the 'death message' than actually seeing a body itself. And I felt the same way. Giving the death message involves going to someone's house, giving them awful news, staying for a little while to answer questions and do your best to support this group of people whose world you might have just shattered, and then leaving them in that state. Once you've found a dead body, you can't really do anything to make its day worse.

But anyway, you don't want to hear about this stuff. Let's get to the body.

My first dead body on the job was the sudden death of an elderly lady. Her (grown up) children had found her and called the ambulance, who in turn called us (so I was spared having to give the death message). Because it was a sudden death, a sergeant had to attend too – so Fara attended with me. I was on high alert for the whole of the job to make sure I was being as caring and empathetic as I could possibly be, mainly by keeping the family informed of everything that was going on and why it was happening. For their part, they were obviously sad and shocked, but they managed to stay calm through the whole thing.

The first thing we had to do was go and inspect the body. That involved putting on the white CSI suits that you see in the movies. The woman was laid on her bed, with a bad cut on her leg. The ambulance crew had determined that the cause of death was likely blood loss from the cut, and we were inclined to agree.

I wasn't exactly upset to see the body, but it didn't feel right. The parallels with my grandparents were, in some respects, quite striking – an elderly person, with me by their bedside. But of course, I didn't know this lady at all. It just felt weird. But I pushed through – we had a job to do.

The death did not seem immediately suspicious, but it also wasn't obvious how the woman had sustained the injury – there wasn't anything sharp lying about or anything that might have caused the cut. So we called CSI to come and examine the scene, and in the meantime we went back downstairs and started on the paperwork. We had to take statements from the family, of course, and we had our own lengthy forms to fill in which required information from a variety of sources and systems.

With the paperwork done, all that was left to do was wait for CSI to come. We were a few hours into the job at this point – and flies were starting to come in and sit on the body. I shut the windows to keep them out – but then we had to contend with the smell that had started to materialise. I deemed the smell better than the flies – for the victim's dignity, if not our own sensibilities.

A man from CSI arrived and started to take pictures. His main goals were to capture the scene in detail, and assist us in identifying how the woman sustained the injury and whether a third party was involved. If a third party was involved, we would be looking at a potential murder or manslaughter case.

As he was on his own, my sergeant and I had to help the CSI guy do a survey of the body. That meant looking for anything out of the ordinary – additional injuries that might indicate a struggle, for example. We had to roll the body over to look at both sides and the back, which released a deeply unpleasant smell that was unmistakeably the stench of a dead body. One of her hands was clenched; we had to slowly pry it open, fighting the rigor mortis that had set in. Then I had to systematically touch and feel over her face, skull and neck to see if there was any perceivable injury there.

It felt incredibly wrong to be disturbing the body of the woman like this. I knew why we were doing it, and got on with the job, but every fibre in my body was screaming 'let her rest in peace!'

Throughout the process, Fara kept looking at me.

"Are you ok?" she asked.

"Yep," I replied. A few minutes later, she asked again.

"Are you *sure* you're ok?"

Afterwards, the CSI guy took more photos from various places of the house. Together, we constructed a rough timeline of events. The key thing, though, was that all three of us – the CSI guy, Fara, and me – were satisfied that there was no third party involvement and therefore no crime had been committed. Instead, it was likely to have been a tragic accident. Based on the evidence, my guess is that the woman had fallen and hit her leg on a piece of furniture. Given the frailty of the skin that comes with age, the cut would have bled profusely.

The job took the vast majority of my shift. Once we got back to the station and it was time to clock out, Fara told me that I could call her over my rest days if I needed to talk about today.

I appreciated her support, but it was a bit strange. There are many areas in policing where you're supposed to just suck things up – but when you see a dead body, everyone suddenly starts treating you like you'll burst into flame at any moment. I guess it's because there's something very primal about seeing death that everyone can easily understand might be upsetting to a person. But in all honesty, I was more shaken after my Wexham Park assault suspect had verbally abused me for over half an hour in the back of a police van than I'd been by seeing the dead body.

Speaking of him, progress on that case had sadly ground to a halt. I'd been to an initial hearing a little while back; other officers only ever went to hearings if they were required to give evidence, but I thought it would be a good learning experience for me. On the day of the hearing, I was at Reading Magistrate's court – only to find out that the hearing had been postponed. The defence wanted to provide evidence that the suspect had mental health issues, but needed more time to build their case – so things got postponed. This sort of thing was extremely common, and was the reason why officers almost never attend hearings unless they had to.

Since then, we'd had a few more rescheduled hearings, and nothing else. I was still trying to keep the victims updated. Even though my obligation to update them ends after the charge, I felt they deserved to know that they were getting justice. Those updates became harder and harder to give; how could I let them know they would get justice when nothing was happening?

CHAPTER 29

BREAKDOWN

Though I was fine looking at dead bodies, in a more general sense I most definitely was not fine. The combination of exhaustion, frustration, and mental load was really starting to take its toll on me.

During my rotation in ICR, the stress and pressure mainly affected my physical health. I got ill a lot because my immune system was not functioning as well as it should have because I was exhausted due to sleep deprivation and constant stress. Though I never worked such a physically demanding shift pattern again, the pace of the work in my subsequent rotations meant that I never really recovered from those ten weeks.

Then, in PCT, I was learning a completely different skillset – and coming to terms with the fact that my detective training at Sully had barely prepared me for doing investigation work. There were long, late nights in PCT, and new skills to be learnt from scratch. And then, of course, just as I was starting to settle in, everything changed and I took the decision to move to CID since Ali was leaving PCT.

CID was just as much of a learning curve as PCT or ICR had been – but with crimes of a far more serious nature, and with a tutor who didn't seem to want anything to do with me. I've mentioned it before, but the sink-or-swim feeling didn't leave me for a long time. It might have been because I was changing departments so often that I never had time to get my feet under the table, as it were.

Whatever the cause, I perpetually felt like I was behind my peers, and not doing good police work as much as just trying to survive and keep my head above water. It was mentally exhausting. On top of that, I still felt somewhat bitter that Sully hadn't trained us to actually do the job we signed up to do. If the training had reflected what happened out in the real world, and included all the things you actually needed to get through a day of police work, I'm sure that it would have prevented a lot of stress and helplessness – for others as well as me.

Other officers often talked about just being confident as a way to defeat those feelings. Fake it till you make it, as it were. And though I can do that to a degree, I find it incredibly hard. I get confidence from knowing my shit. And that was exactly what I felt like I didn't know 99% of the time.

Often after getting home from work, I would go to bed and just lie there for a while. Looking back, it was a classic case of overwhelm. My brain was burnt out from dealing with my job all day long, and it felt like the only thing I was capable of doing was staying still, in an empty room, with no noise or other stimuli until the sensation passed. It was a feeling I'd never had before. When I was in that state, I was also completely unable to handle social situations. I am the kind of person that enjoys hanging out with friends, though since starting with TVP I'd not had much opportunity to socialise due to my shift patterns. But as my mental health started to degrade, I'd find myself unable to handle interactions with people. Instead, I would throw myself into exercise in an attempt to look after my mind. Running, kickboxing, you name it – if I wasn't working, I was usually doing one of those, or sleeping. On the rare occasions that I scheduled something social, I frequently had to cancel – including a first date (which, needless to say, didn't get rescheduled).

Even when I took a four-day holiday to Italy with a friend, it only took one day back on the job before I felt just as exhausted and overwhelmed as I'd been before the holiday. Looking back, I don't know if my friends fully realised how difficult I was finding the police. And that's because sometimes, on my days off, I was strangely joyful.

My family noticed, though.

"I'm worried about you," my sister said on the phone one evening, "you're not yourself."

My parents came to stay for a while to help me decorate my flat, but also I suspect to check I was OK. I remember it because I was campaigning hard to paint one wall lime green, which my dad was dead against. I got in from work after an early shift and, after I'd told my parents what an awful day it had been, my dad quipped,

"If your day's made you feel miserable, wait until you see your wall!"

He then proudly showed me the lime green feature wall. Needless to say, I actually quite liked it – and his humour helped me feel a bit better about everything.

I mentioned back when I started in ICR that changing out of my blacks and into my civilian clothes became a bit of a ritual that helped me to leave the job at work and enjoy my time off. Though I only wore blacks during my time in ICR, the ritual of leaving work at work became more and more ingrained in my psyche until when I was not at work, it was like work didn't exist at all. I remember that I would get to my days off and think to myself "this is my real life, and I'm going to live it!"

You might be thinking to yourself: what's so bad about that? Sounds like a great coping strategy! And, at first, it was. High-stress work like policing requires a level of compartmentalisation. If you go to bed every night feeling sad about everything that happened, the job will consume you within a week. But as work became more problematic, my refusal to think about work or even accept that it was a part of my life became less of a coping strategy and more of an avoidance strategy. And eventually, even that failed, and I'd find myself bursting into tears for no reason while on my days off as well as at work.

On the days I had to go in to work, I would still essentially be in denial right up until I walked in. With other jobs, I'd spend the commute thinking about work: what calls did I have? What tasks needed doing? Who did I need to speak to? None of that here. And when I walked into the station, a mental switch would flip and I'd go numb on the inside. I'd do my best to focus deeply on the work and avoid the feelings of overwhelm, but it was only ever an hour or so before I was watching the clock, hoping no other incidents would happen that day and that I could go home without overtime.

At the same time, when off duty I was permanently on edge. We'd been told at Sully that, as police officers, we were never off duty. If you're walking on the street on the way to the supermarket and something criminal happens, you're expected to step in. And of course, as someone who has made the choice to work as a police officer, once you have the tools and powers to help you feel motivated to. But nobody ever explained what 'stepping in' looks like, and I suppose different people have different interpretations of that. It might mean calling the police and observing as best you can to give a witness statement, but in other cases it might be to verbally or physically intervene. And the prospect of that was causing me a lot of stress, on top of everything else. Living in a city, where there is always something happening, I noticed that I became hypervigilant. I was easily startled by sounds. I lost count of the number of times I heard a scream while walking in a crowded part of the city, and immediately thought the worst:

Someone is being robbed.

Someone is being assaulted.

Someone is being raped.

When I looked up, alarmed and adrenaline spiking through my system, it was usually just someone shouting at their friend on the other side of the road or something.

And so, during my time at CID, I had to take leave due to stress for the first time. I woke up one morning for my shift, and I simply couldn't stop crying. I called in sick, though I didn't tell them why at that point. I stayed off for two shifts, feeling desperately guilty for being unable to go into work. After all, I'd only been on the force for a little over a year at this point. By police standards, I hadn't seen any really traumatic incidents, dealt with a really sad case, or been physically attacked while carrying out my work. It made me feel that my struggles were on some level unjustified. But I just couldn't go into work when I was crying uncontrollably at the drop of a hat.

After two days, I felt well enough to drag myself into work.

"Hi, Jade," Fara greeted me when she saw me, "feeling better?"

I told her that I wasn't really sure, and confessed to her that I was struggling with my mental health. Fara nodded.

"All right, let's go and have a chat," she said.

And within about five seconds of sitting down, I was in floods of tears again. Fara and my other colleagues were supportive. Fara was kind, but also (in classic police fashion) very procedure-driven. She quickly started talking about putting in place 'actions' on an HR plan to improve the situation. It all felt a bit clinical and like we were just on a job, ticking boxes, reading out standard scripts and going through standardised risk assessments and forms. Another colleague said:

"I was just the same. At one point, I cried every day before coming in, and every day after getting home!" I know she was trying to make me feel better, but I was more shocked that she was still here.

"How did you move past it?" I sniffled as we sat there.

"Oh, it passed when I started caring less," she admitted. I remember thinking to myself at the time: 'how the fuck did you manage to get through those shifts if you felt like this?!'

The inspector probably reacted the best to the whole situation. She didn't start bombarding me with questions or reassurances, or offer me meaningless platitudes. She simply offered me a piece of cake.

"I hate to see anyone upset," she said. And I believed her.

Now that my mental state was out in the open, I was sent home to rest. Before I went, the inspector asked me if I was OK and gave me her number, telling me I could call any time to talk. The empathy and genuine nature of her response was something I still appreciate to this day. My sergeant referred me to the wellbeing coordinator in the force and the employee assistance programme. Esme in particular was really supportive during this (and future) time off due to stress.

The TVP wellbeing team were a funny lot. Some were dedicated wellbeing specialists, others were regular officers who had taken on an extra role. Their role, unsurprisingly, was to look after the wellbeing of the force. They also had a fund that sergeants could apply to if they had an idea for improving the wellbeing of their team. I remember that once we got money to go on a team day out. An outdoor activity followed by a pub meal. I personally didn't want to go; I felt like I spent enough time with my team as it was, and although I didn't dislike them, I also didn't feel like I had anything in common with them. Down at the pub, I knew we'd have nothing to talk about. However, there wasn't much of a choice. I couldn't just take the day off – if I chose not to go to the event, I would likely have been expected to work instead. And if I'd done that, it would have made me look desperate to avoid my team, which would have been very awkward.

That day was very representative of the wellbeing team's efforts: a nice gesture, but not a very effective one. People were still miserable. Another time, someone came into our office and told us that the wellbeing team had left free snacks on the table in the kitchen downstairs. We all went downstairs to have a look at the freebies. They consisted of a few cardboard boxes with crisps, chocolate bars, biscuits and candies. Again, although I appreciated the gesture I didn't see how a few cheap and unhealthy snacks were going to improve anyone's wellbeing.

I was, and am, convinced that the whole 'wellbeing strategy' at TVP was completely wrong. Instead of treating the root causes of the force's wellbeing problems – a lack of training, poor office and IT equipment, severe understaffing that put too much pressure on officers, and an overall low feeling of appreciation or job satisfaction – they were instead trying to treat the symptoms with lacklustre solutions like free bags of crisps and trips to the pub. Perhaps these were the efforts of officers doing the wellbeing job in their spare time. It would explain why their efforts were so meagre; the people in charge of our wellbeing were just as burnt out and unhappy as the rest of us, and likely hadn't been given any training or guidance on how to achieve the job – just a budget and an order to "cheer everyone up a bit."

Anyway, back to my story. I prepared to leave the office, mortified at my tear-streaked face and hoping that nobody noticed me.

"Do you need any other support?" Fara asked me before I left.

The question stuck in my head because I couldn't give her an answer. Deep down, I was starting to realise that the only way out of feeling like this was to leave the job. I know that many of the other DC DHEP graduates who quit did so for similar reasons. The daily grind of boring admin, the poor work environment, the stress of not knowing what to do most of the time and not having been trained properly, and most of all the complete lack of satisfaction from the work. They all became too much after a while.

Another time in the office, I remember I ran into an old colleague on the stairs.

"How are you?" I said.

"Living the dream," came the ritual reply.

I gave him a faint smile, but in that moment it suddenly dawned on me that I was in fact living my dream. And it was nothing like I thought it would be. In fact, it had left me feeling worse than I'd ever felt before. I couldn't just give up on that dream, could I? I'd been working for it for what felt like forever, and I'd never wanted to do a job as much as I'd wanted to do this. I couldn't just give up on that because of this setback.

But, try as I might, when Fara asked me if I need any more support, I couldn't think of a single thing anyone could say or do to make things better for me.

CHAPTER 30

LEAVING CID

The actions on my wellbeing plan were fairly basic things that everyone is instructed to do to try and help improve their mood: eating healthy, doing exercise, and getting enough sleep. I did my best with them. Eating healthily wasn't a problem, and exercise was by this point pretty much all I did outside of work. Sleeping well wasn't entirely in my control, but since I had left the ICR night shifts behind it was at least vaguely achievable.

None of it really helped. I found myself starting to break down in tears more regularly, just like the rest of my team. As time went by, I cared less and less whether anyone saw me leaving or arriving with a tear-streaked face. I took more time off for stress, during which Fara and others called me frequently to ask if I needed more support. It was kind of them, but in those moments all I really wanted was for them to just leave me be.

And then, suddenly, things came to a pretty unpleasant head.

I'd just returned to work after another few days off with stress, and during a charging process that I was going through with my tutor (a rare occurrence) it became apparent that I'd made some mistakes. They weren't huge; there weren't any major repercussions, but I think I got a bit of a wigging from the custody sergeant. As was her way, my tutor remained silent through the whole thing and didn't offer me any help at all.

"That can't ever happen again," was all she said to me as we left custody. "You made both of us look bad. I'm not here to babysit you; you're still on your probation."

I did my best to ignore how nonsensical that statement was, especially coming from my fucking tutor. But, shortly after we got back to our station, I found myself in a meeting with sergeant Fara over the issue.

"I've had some feedback from your tutor," she told me in a serious tone. She then read me some of the highlights of that feedback. It was a bit like a dam had burst; after months of ignoring me and dismissing me as unimportant, she'd finally decided to weigh in on my progress with a pretty damning verbal report to my sergeant. Listening to what she'd said, you'd think it was a miracle I'd managed to make it through basic training, let alone any of the time I'd spent at Slough.

I can't say I was surprised to learn how my tutor felt, but I was fairly amazed that she'd decided to pour all this out to my sergeant. She'd not told me any of this, so that I could address any of what she felt I was doing wrong. It felt completely vindictive, and I told Fara so. I also told her about the incident with the charging process, and the uses of words like 'babysit' and 'probation' which were unnecessarily aggressive and unprofessional.

Sergeant Fara accepted my side of the argument, but without giving away whether she agreed with me or my tutor. Fara was often inscrutable like that.

The inspector, by contrast, came to find me once Fara had filled her in on the situation and told me that she thought my tutor's conduct was unacceptable. As it turned out, her support didn't really do much to change events, but it did mean a lot to me in the moment to know that someone cared about me and accepted my side of the story.

Fara suggested a three-way mediation session between her, me, and my tutor. I was open to it, but I told Fara I did not want to do it today as emotions had run very high today. Everyone needed to cool off a little first.

My tutor and I didn't speak again after that. We settled for some uncomfortable silences in the office and avoiding each other. And, before we could get the meeting set up, I was sent off on a four-week CID course as part of my training.

The CID course, as it was informally known, was a course meant for all investigators in the force. It was taught at Sully, and it was with relief that I returned to the small rooms of Imbert Court. I felt relieved to have some breathing space away from CID.

If it felt like a long time since attending my SACCI course, my time as a fresh trainee felt an eternity ago. The differences between then and now couldn't have been more striking. During initial training I was full of excitement and enthusiasm for the job, and a determination to do my best and make a difference. Now things felt much more sombre. I distinctly remember thinking to myself that I couldn't picture any kind of positive future after the CID course back at the station. But despite all of that, I was looking forward to the course. Sully felt safe and familiar. It was somewhere I could just focus on my own development and learn from my mistakes without any repercussions.

I was also pleased to get a chance to catch up with my fellow DC DHEPers, and some new faces on their own paths to becoming detectives. We all enjoyed the chance to socialise in the evenings without the pressure of work looming in the background. Sometimes, we even managed to get out to a nearby pub – somewhat paradoxically, it felt like a detox.

There was a lot of venting during those evenings. Everyone had experiences and issues that were bothering them, which I found sort of encouraging – it wasn't just me. But it was always hard to gauge how other people were doing; the habit of projecting confidence and playing your cards close to your chest meant you could never be quite sure how much things were bothering other people.

The course itself was taught by a main trainer, but consisted mostly of guest lectures from police staff and officers from various departments. We heard from intelligence teams, covert operations, a CPS lawyer, and a sexual offences expert among others. The variety was exciting, but the format of sitting and listening to people talk from 9 to 5 each day was not the most stimulating way to learn. Still, I relentlessly made notes which I then typed up in the evening so I could make sense of everything I'd heard.

Relatively early into the course, I saw an email from sergeant Fara back at Slough. I'd been pulled up again – this time for not progressing a case. In truth, I had progressed the case – I just hadn't done a very small amount of paperwork that was needed to finish things off. The tone of sergeant Fara's email was incredibly accusatory and aggressive. And it was the last straw. I was no longer on speaking terms with my tutor, and now my sergeant was taking a swing at me. I was sick of Slough CID.

I went to see the course coordinator, and essentially told them that there was no way in hell that I would go back to Slough CID. After explaining my situation and how I was feeling, the course coordinator accepted my position – and that was the end of my stint in CID. After the course, I was going to head to the Domestic Abuse Investigation Unit, or DAIU.

I can't exactly say that I was excited by this news – I was far too burnt out and stressed to feel that – but I was looking forward to the fresh start. I'd heard that there was more of a victim-focus in DAIU, which appealed to me, as did the chance to make a real impact with the cases I worked on. So I threw myself into the training, trying to absorb all the information I could. I thought to myself: 'I've got four weeks of rest. Let's see if I can clarify some of the things that don't make sense to me, get some new knowledge and skills, and start again at DAIU.' Deep down, I knew that DAIU was my last chance to make things work.

Just like the previous course, I was in my element in the classroom. I did my best to absorb all information and facts from the course – so it was unfortunate that, once again, the content we were learning about was relevant but purely theoretical most of the time. The knowledge I needed the most back at my station was practical knowledge about process, procedures and administration. It was all the things you actually need to get through a case. My heart sank as I realised I was still going to have to rely on asking colleagues for help, or trial and error, to discover the quirks of the system and unwritten rules that would help make my life materially easier as an officer.

Even when we did touch on practical things, the mismatch between what we were taught at Sully and the things we were told at the station was as big as it was during our initial training. The example that stands out to me was from our sexual offences input. The specialist told us explicitly that we should not agree to be OIC for a rape case if we'd not done the special sexual offences course. They explained this could jeopardise the case in court if the defence clocked that the OIC was not trained to deal with rapes. However, it wasn't very far into my time in DAIU that my sergeant asked me to be OIC in a rape case. When I explained what we'd been told in training, my sergeant explained that no one in the team was trained and that therefore he was left with no choice but to allocate the case to someone. He assured me I would not be blamed for it and that the senior officers at the station were in agreement.

Stuff like this annoyed the hell out of me. Couldn't our trainers and our station commanders just talk amongst themselves and make sure that the stuff they were teaching us was actually what we'd be expected to do in our jobs?

Another example was the topic of arresting people for breaching pre-charge bail conditions. Remember that? As a reminder, pre-charge bail conditions aren't enforceable, so we were instructed not to arrest suspects for breaching them. But during the domestic abuse training at Sully, the trainers deeply impressed on us how important it was to make those arrests because not taking action would likely make the victim feel very disillusioned and unsafe. I agreed completely, but I also knew that this was not our decision to make as DCs.

Since I was going to DAIU, I decided to challenge the trainers on this one. I asked them if they could please speak to the sergeants and inspectors throughout the force or even the strategy team to update the procedure on this, because we would just be given different instructions the moment we got back to our stations.

"Yes, don't worry, the sergeants are aware of what we're covering in this input too," the trainers said. And that was all that was ever said on the topic. I simply shrugged and wrote it off in my head as another broken aspect of our training. I think that was the moment that I gave up on the idea of changing things for the better.

As I said, the CID course involved a lot of classroom training. As the course went on it became apparent that there was going to be no practical training on the course.

"Couldn't we just do an op day again but as DCs?" one of my course mates wondered out loud. "That would be super useful, wouldn't it?"

I agreed. Things like managing a live incident, which we covered briefly via a PowerPoint presentation, is not something you can learn from a PowerPoint presentation. You need to practice it. The training school would have been a safe environment to do that practice, and we knew that they could make it happen – we'd done our op days during initial training, after all. But unfortunately, this was just not the way training was done.

Towards the end of the course, we had an input from a defence barrister. As part of the class, several students would also be cross-examined by him to get a feel for what being cross-examined in court is like. Cross examination, in case you're not sure, is when a witness is questioned by the opposing party during a trial (for instance, when a witness for the defence is questioned by the prosecution). The purpose is to challenge the credibility of the witness by identifying holes in their story or contradictions.

By the second day of the barrister's input, everyone was getting nervous about the prospect of being put on the spot and ripped to pieces by this guy, who was an experienced barrister. The trainer spent the whole day placating everyone by reassuring us that there was nothing to worry about and that it was really not as bad as we were imaging it was going to be. I was first up, being cross-examined about a real statement from an arrest I had made.

The trainer lied through his teeth. It was bad.

"Ms Cameron," the defence barrister began, "to enforce the law, you need to know the law. Do you agree?"

"I do," I replied.

"Can you please tell the court what legislation is being quoted on top of the police statement?" he then asked.

I was, needless to say, unable to answer. It was a piece of writing that I'd never been taught about, and certainly never thought much about. On a witness statement form, the witness statement is the important bit, not the legislation around it.

"In your witness statement," he continued, "you wrote 'we drove to 123 High Street'. Is that correct?"

"Yes," I replied, but much more nervously now than before.

"Are you sure about that?" he asked.

"I am," I replied

"So you agree, Ms Cameron, that you and your colleague drove to 123 High Street separately?"

"Um, no," I replied, "My colleague drove, I was in the driver's seat."

"But Ms Cameron, 'we drove' means that you both drove, which means that you came separately. Are you saying that your statement is incorrect?"

And on it went. What struck me the most about the process was how easy it was to make someone look incompetent with a certain line of questioning. Even though I'd not made mistakes in my statement or my investigation, his questioning made it seem to a jury as though I had got things wrong and didn't know what I was talking about. Another thing that struck me was that all the questions were about things that were barely related to the case. Logically, of course, my inability to describe the legislation on top of the statement had no bearing on my reliability as a witness – but because he'd picked on it in his questioning, it suddenly seemed relevant to the case.

I sat down, expecting to get some sympathy and a 'you'll do better next time' from the trainer, barrister, and my classmates. But to my surprise, my feedback was positive. Apparently, this is just the way it goes. Part of the point of the experience was to get you used to not being in control. The barrister will try and make you look foolish, and you can't stop it. All you can do is answer their questions, stay as calm as you can, and not get flustered.

So, four weeks passed, we received our certificates, and said our goodbyes. I went back home with a curious mix of feelings. On the one hand, I felt satisfied with some of the new things I'd learned – and I was incredibly relieved to be moving on from CID to DAIU. I summoned my courage and called my tutor, with the aim of explaining that I'd be moving on and to try and bury the hatchet. She didn't answer – and never replied to the message I sent. Never mind, I thought. On to the next.

On the other hand, the course had brought back all my dissatisfaction with our training and how little it prepared us for the real world of policing. This course had been no different – so what would happen in DAIU? I was determined to do my best, come what may. But hanging over it all was my mental health – and that was hanging by a thread.

PART 5

DOMESTIC ABUSE INVESTIGATION UNIT

CHAPTER 31

WELCOME TO DAIU

As you might expect, the Domestic Abuse Investigation Unit, or DAIU, investigates domestic abuse cases – but not all of them. DAIU only deals with the high-risk domestic abuse cases; cases that are classified as either medium or standard risk are dealt with by other teams. In a rare example of police bureaucracy and victim care actually working with each other, there were no low-risk domestic abuse cases.

The DAIU office was in Windsor, which was a nice change of scene from Slough police station. I walked in on my first day feeling nervous (nothing new there). As with CID, I was feeling nervous because of the nature of the cases I'd be dealing with. Was I ready to be handling such serious cases? I hoped so. On the plus side, I was optimistic that DAIU would be the right place for me. In DAIU there's a heavy focus on the victims and on building a close relationship with them. I'd previously worked in the victim support sector, which did give me a level of confidence that I hadn't felt in other departments.

Having been in the police for well over a year now, I already knew how cases made it to our department. You remember those Dash risk assessments (also known as a DOM5) that ICR officers have to complete every time they go to a DA case? Those forms end with a grading of standard, medium or high risk, which the officer at the scene decides on based on the questions and their best judgement about the risk of the case. The decision is reviewed by their sergeant, and if the sergeant agrees that a case is high risk then it is forwarded to DAIU.

I'd always found the risk assessment process tricky. Even though you're using a standardised form, there's still plenty of room for subjectivity and gut feel in there. When I was in ICR, my concept of risk was fairly in line with the general public's – which meant that any time someone disclosed something to me about domestic abuse, loud alarm bells started ringing in my head. I remember one example from the first few weeks of ICR. I spoke with a lady in her 40s who sat in the office crying, telling us that her husband wouldn't allow her to do anything. They'd been together for over 20 years, but now she was ready to leave him. The husband was currently abroad, and her plan was to pack her bags and move out before he got home, staying with a friend until she could get herself established.

I was shocked by the story. I was also very worried that the husband would go into a frenzy when he returned. We were taught that a victim leaving the perpetrator was the most dangerous time in a DA case because the perpetrator felt they'd lost control, and was likely to use violence to try and reassert control.

After we'd done the Dash risk assessment with the lady, talked about next steps, and she'd left the station, Jay turned around to me.

"What do you think? What risk is it?"

"High," I replied instantly. Jay smiled.

"Why is that?" he asked. I explained my rationale to him and what I'd learnt in training school. Once I'd finished, he simply replied:

"Forget training school. This is medium at best. Trust me, DAIU wouldn't look at this in a million years." I was surprised, but (as usual) he was right. The reviewing sergeant set the case at medium risk, and it was handled in ICR.

Interestingly, once a case was passed to DAIU, they would review it and decide whether they agreed with the grading. If they didn't, they had the power to regrade the risk level of a case, effectively bouncing it back to ICR. I always thought it was a bit unusual that ICR handled DA cases. Medium risk cases can still be very intense; I never really understood how a response officer could have the time or energy to handle a case like that. In some stations in TVP, I think standard and medium risk cases were passed on to PCT, but that wasn't the case at Slough while I was there.

You'll not be surprised to learn, of course, that often DAIU did not agree with the ratings given to DA cases. The same ownership battles that I saw played out in PCT and CID took place in DAIU as well. As you already know, PCT would try to bounce cases by arguing that they weren't burglaries or robberies. Generally, the only ways CID could bounce cases was by arguing that there was a close family connection or intimate relationship between offender and victim, which then made it a case for DAIU, or an offence involving a child which could be forwarded to the child abuse investigation unit (CAIU).

For DAIU's part, the arguments tended to be about the nature of the relationship. 'No, no they only met once. How can they be in an intimate relationship? It's not for us to deal with.' Of course, every department would take advantage of the grey area around what constitutes an intimate partner, which wasn't helped by the often-conflicting information in the case records. But in everyone's defence, too, it was often very hard to categorise things accurately. When talking about risk, there is so much room for subjectivity, and often DAIU officers relied much more on their own judgement than on the score when grading a case. After a while I started to get a feel for which cases were high and which were not, though I often found it difficult to put that feeling into words.

From my very first day, I noticed that this was a predominantly female department – though the sergeants were all male at the time. To my relief, the welcome at DAIU was far warmer than it had been at any of my previous departments. People went out of their way to introduce themselves to me, and I was included in the tea round straight away. With my nerves and confidence in relative tatters after CID, the team feeling I got from DAIU was a little bit like a life raft I could climb into and recover. The location change helped, too. I was also pleased to find that the skills and experience I had picked up so far meant that I wasn't starting entirely from scratch this time. I actually had something to bring to the team instead of being a clueless burden. I didn't even particularly need to rely on my tutor in DAIU, a nice guy about my age who we'll call Brian. Brian left the department about four months after I'd arrived, and sent me a really supportive message saying that he believed I had the right skills to be a great DC. That was a great little boost for me.

However, the gossip machine was working at extra high speeds in DAIU. Every department was a hotbed of gossip, but in DAIU it was something else. Every conversation over a cup of coffee or at lunch was about the goings-on in the station.

'Which officer cheated with another officer?'

'Who's being investigated by the professional standards department?'

'Who's been promoted?'

The length at which my colleagues could talk about these things was incredible. To save my sanity, I would sometimes throw in a conversation topic I found interesting – a specific case, perhaps, or a new type of technology being used in police forces – but usually they'd only get a few nods or yes/no answers before being dropped completely.

Apropos of nothing, one of the sergeants at DAIU had particularly deep bags under his eyes, and moved and reacted to things noticeably slower than the rest of us; I got the impression that he was extremely fatigued and close to collapse. The officers on his team seemed to compensate for him by being especially vocal and high-energy; I could never quite escape the mental image of a coop full of loud and hyperactive hens surrounding one tired and defeated rooster.

Given the gossip machine's ability to instantly spread information across the entire station, I was sure that everyone at DAIU knew exactly why I was with them. It wasn't unheard of for DC DHEP students to do a rotation in DAIU, but I don't think it was that common for them to arrive at DAIU after having a breakdown and refusing to work in CID anymore. Given that everyone was being pretty pleasant to me – and it felt genuine – I decided that whatever gossip was going on about me behind my back, it couldn't be that bad – so I resolved to just do my best to get on with the job.

CHAPTER 32

THE POLICE AGENDA, AGAIN

In DAIU we often used a type of record on Niche called a risk management occurrence, or RMO. RMOs didn't record crimes, but instead noted any safeguarding and risk-related information about a specific individual. In DAIU there was a policy that after an investigation had finished, we would continue to contact the high-risk victim every month for a year to check in. The idea behind this is that it would help to build a stronger, more trusting relationship between officers and victims, which would not only help victims feel more supported but hopefully encourage them to share and report further incidents, helping us keep them safer.

A nice idea – but I quickly discovered that, like so many other police procedures, the idea had lost something in the execution. The reality was that nearly every RMO contact felt very forced, largely because we had to call whether the victim wanted us to or not. I remember one call where the woman on the other end of the call lost her patience.

"Oh my god! This is ridiculous! Stop calling me!" she yelled at me before hanging up the phone.

I didn't disagree with her; it was ridiculous. But if we didn't write a monthly update on the Niche record, we could be in trouble. The police agenda reared its head again, and – as it always did – it didn't just ignore the victim's agenda, it actively got in the way of what victims wanted. And because none of us wanted to risk getting disciplined or even fired, we put up with it and called people who did not want to be called. And because the 12-month limit on an RMO was reset if another incident was reported, it was technically possible to end up badgering a victim who didn't want contact with us for years.

Don't get me wrong; I liked the idea of staying in touch with victims, and the aims behind the RMO. But as soon as it turned into a bureaucratic checklist that didn't take into account a victim's individual circumstances and wishes, it quickly felt forced for both officer and victim. In the case of the woman who shouted down the phone at me, after discussing it with my colleagues I decided not to call again.

I also discovered an altogether more heartbreaking aspect of these DA cases. I was calling a victim as per their RMO to check in. She was in her early twenties, and I asked her how things were going.

"Is there anything you'd like to discuss with me?"

"No," she said to me bluntly, "I will never speak to the police again. After I reported that assault a few weeks ago they took away our baby. All I want is my baby back. Nothing more."

She wasn't alone. More often than not, victims who were parents wouldn't want to disclose any abuse to the police for fear that their children would be taken away.

I completely understood the sentiment. Any information shared with police will also be shared with social services via a MASH or a MARAC, and they may decide it's in the best interests of the child to take them out of the home, either temporarily or permanently. Because it wasn't a police decision, and we had to share the information with social services, I could never give victims assurances that this wouldn't happen. So for a lot of victims, the police became the enemy and they were determined to lie to us to avoid separation from their children. It was an awful dynamic.

In my experience, the only times where regular calls were appreciated by victims were when those calls weren't mandated by an RMO. I often gave victims that I spoke to my business card and told them they could talk to me if they wanted to, and on occasion they did contact me. Even if I wasn't OIC for their case, I'd always try to help them as quickly as possible. If I could give them the information they were asking for, then I would. I wouldn't just pass it on to the OIC without first listening to them or trying to assist. In my mind, this was the attitude that the senior ranks were trying to instil in the force through all the strategies and plans to improve victim satisfaction.

I remember one instance where I was tasked to do a Dash risk assessment with a victim. I went to her house and completed the assessment – but I also listened to her as she told me all about the case and her ex-partner. She told me that she felt really unsafe in her house and desperately wanted to move; she was speaking to the housing association about it. It was clear that the woman needed to get this stuff off her chest; I responded by listening to her and not rushing the appointment, despite the workload I had waiting for me. The emotion and feeling in her voice told me how important it was to her that she tell me her story.

Once she was done, I gave her my card and said she could call me or email me with questions. I also told her that I would stay in touch with her; as the case was high risk, the victim would be getting her own RMO and the person who completed the risk assessment (me) would keep contacting her every month.

However, upon reading the risk assessment my sergeant regraded the case as medium risk which meant there would be no RMO. That meant there was no duty to call every month – but I ended up speaking to her frequently anyway. I gave her updates on her case, including outcomes at court, and even ended up writing a housing letter for her and sending it to her housing association.

My colleagues told me to just drop it – it wasn't my job anymore. It was the typical attitude of any officer; once something wasn't your job, you left it well alone. I suppose I might have resented my colleagues for that attitude, but honestly, I didn't. In part, they were trying to protect me from overworking, and in part they were just products of the institution that is policing. But I strongly felt that it was an important part of my job. This was a domestic abuse victim; I was part of the domestic abuse team. I'd told her I was going to be in touch with her, and it wasn't her fault that the case got regraded – that was on us. Why should she suddenly get silence from the police just because we'd decided she wasn't high risk? I couldn't justify that to myself. Besides, victim support was one of the only good bits about my job – that chance to look after someone who is vulnerable, scared, and in need of support. There was no way I wasn't going to do it.

At the end of the case, I was pleased to receive genuine appreciation from the victim for my help. These were the kinds of interactions where I really felt I helped someone, even though it was in a small way. And I feel good about these. I feel good about taking responsibility and not dropping the ball as soon as it was no longer viewed as 'my job'.

CHAPTER 33

SETTLING INTO DAIU

My first three months in DAIU were actually a bit of a whirlwind where I got stuck into a wide variety of things that are worth mentioning here.

Pretty early on, I attended hospital to pick up a DA victim and take her to her house to pack. Her husband was currently in police custody, but as you know that means we could only keep him for 24 hours. So in that time, the victim was leaving home to go to a refuge. I wasn't sure why the woman was in hospital – I don't think it was connected to the DA case – but either way, when we got there we found this poor middle-aged woman in a quite understandable state of distress. She was all over the place emotionally, and interestingly wouldn't stop talking.

I was attending with my tutor Brian, and it became apparent very quickly that he didn't really know what to do with this woman. But my experience in victim support kicked in, and so I ended up taking charge while Brian faded into the background. I marshalled this woman into our car, back to her house, and all around her house getting her packed up.

"Have you packed a toothbrush?"

"You'll want to take this with you."

"Don't take that, you won't have room for it."

I remember really enjoying the job, despite the unpleasant circumstances that surrounded it. I was doing something I was good at: helping people in crisis. It made me feel like I was doing something right – and, I thought, if DAIU was like this, then I was in the right place.

I also spoke to a teenager about nude images she had shared with a friend. Her mother had made a report to the police after her daughter had told her that she'd shared the images with a boy, who had then shared them with his friends. Since that call, though, the girl had changed her story and was adamant that she hadn't shared the images with the boy.

Brian was not enthusiastic about this job.

"I don't want to go and speak to a teen about nudes on their phone," he complained.

After speaking with the girl, who confirmed her story that she had never sent the images to the boy, we went to go and speak with him. He also denied having the images – so all we could do was give him a document telling him that, if he *did* have any images, that would constitute child pornography and he would need to delete them immediately. We then went back to the girl to give her advice about sharing images online.

It was a strange case. It wasn't clear at all whether there was a crime that everyone was lying about, or if there really was nothing going on. But since nobody was talking, all we could do was give crime prevention advice. And despite Brian's reluctance, I was happy that we'd been able to do that – it's always better to prevent a crime than investigate one.

As an aside, with cases involving nude images and children it's not always in the public interest to treat it as a crime. Consider two underage people, consensually sharing nude images of themselves with each other, where nobody shares the images onwards. Technically, that's still child pornography and therefore a crime. However, no distress has been caused, and neither party has used the images to cause harm to the other. If the case was to be pursued, it would cause a lot of distress to both the children in question, and their families, and neither party would feel that they had received justice at the end of it.

Obviously, the incident in my story would have been in the public interest to pursue, since the girl had alleged that the boy had shared the images on with his friends. But that's not always the case. Whether the police treat an incident as a crime or not, they'll always provide advice to the young people concerned about the risks of making and sharing photos like that.

I also did a day's attachment with the CSI team. One day I just decided it would be good to do. It would be interesting, and it would give me an insight into how CSI worked, which might help me work better with them in my day-to-day work. My sergeant agreed and signed it off – so I spent a day with an officer from CSI.

The day was spent at a house a burglar had visited. I got to do that classic cop show activity, dusting for prints. I was just watching at first, but the CSI officer was very happy for me to join in – she had a whole house to do, after all. If you're curious, dusting for prints is done with a very fine powder that sticks to the oils and moisture components of what's known as a latent print (that means an invisible print, as opposed to a fingerprint left in blood or paint or similar). The print can then be photographed and sometimes lifted. Sadly, we didn't find any prints.

We also had a go at trying to lift a boot print from the carpet via electrostatic lifting – possibly because the CSI officer want to show off the technique to me since I was on attachment. Electrostatic lifting works by placing a sheet over the print, and applying a charge to it. The charge attracts dust and loose dirt from the floor to the film, which gives you the print. Unfortunately, that didn't work either – but it was interesting.

A rather sad moment from those three months came when I worked on a suspected kidnap. The victim's grandmother and aunt came to the police station with the following story: two children had gone to an Eastern European country with their parents. After a few days, the grandmother and aunt got a call from the mother who was in distress. She said that though she thought they'd been going on holiday, the husband was refusing to return to the UK and was keeping the children there. She also accused him of beating her. The grandmother and aunt, understandably, came to us.

We spent hours gathering every scrap of evidence we could. We even got a face-to-face interpreter in so that we could get their statements as accurately as possible. The two women shared plenty of photos of the mother and the two children. In the end the two women spent half a day at the station. After that, we sent a notification to Interpol to say that we believed the woman was in distress and needed help.

A day later, Interpol came back to us. The police in the country in question had sent local units to speak to the woman. She said she was fine, and they would be taking no further action.

That was it. There was nothing else we could do, except tell the family and let them know that we wouldn't be taking any further action. Needless to say, I was not looking forward to that conversation.

The grandmother and aunt, understandably, were very upset, angry and not reassured at all. They didn't hold the police in that country in high regard – and I was inclined to agree with them, especially on the topic of DA. We had no way of telling whether the woman had been speaking to the police with her husband hovering over her shoulder, or if they'd even spoken to her at all.

Unfortunately for me they vented their anger on me and the police in general. We'd let them down, how could we not help, didn't we care? I understood where they were coming from and completely sympathised, but there was nothing else I could do. You can't police a jurisdiction outside your country, so if the police in that jurisdiction won't take action, you're stuck. In the end, I did discover that I could flag the family on our system so that if they re-entered the country we'd know about it – but that was a pretty slim hope. I have no idea what happened to the woman or her children.

What struck me about this case was that, about five minutes after it had finished, the rest of the team had moved on. Compartmentalisation is vital in this job, but this was detachment to a degree that I couldn't wrap my head around. I remember wondering whether I was the only one who cared what happened with this at all?

I was also sent to a strategy meeting in my first three months – or a strat meeting, as they are known – which was a relative disaster. Strat meetings are similar to the MARAC meetings we discussed earlier: a gathering of relevant agencies to discuss a case. Strat meetings were generally about cases involving children, and included social services and schools frequently. I was sent to this meeting because the OIC wasn't available.

"I can go, but I don't know anything about the case," I said to my sergeant.

"Oh, don't worry!" came the usual response. "Just read through the case notes. Call's in 30 minutes."

So I did the best I could in the time I had, and I logged in to the call. The very first question was to me.

"Officer Cameron, can you just run us through the histories of Jim and Barbara, please?"

There were no Jims or Barbaras in the case notes at all. We were one question in, and I was stuck. I felt so embarrassed.

I explained to the attendees that I wasn't the OIC on the case, that they weren't available, and asked the others to continue while I looked up the relevant information. I don't think anyone minded too much, but it was still so embarrassing and unprofessional. And, I thought, completely avoidable if I'd not been chucked into this call with barely any time at all to prepare. Very frustrating.

A more satisfying incident: I prepared for the release of a high-risk DA offender. I'd not worked on any cases involving him beforehand, but I knew he was a nasty offender. The victim had a restraining order against him, but we were confident that he was going to breach it – he had done so many times in the past.

Our preparations had two main prongs. The first was to find out about him. Where was he being released to? Did he have access to a vehicle that we could log on the ANPR system? Who was his probation officer? What were the terms of his probation?

The second was to get in touch with his victim. Did she know about this? How was she coping? Where was she based? What were her plans? We also flagged her address in Niche, so that if we ever got a call from that address the officers responding would know that a high-risk DA victim was at the address and an urgent response was needed.

The victim, surprisingly, was fairly calm about things. She shared our certainty that he would breach his restraining order, and had taken the precaution of buying a Ring doorbell so that she would have evidence if he came onto the property. And sure enough, about two weeks after his release, he arrived at her property and started shouting at her and threatening her. She called the police, they descended, and based on that and the evidence from the doorbell, he went back to prison. I remember thinking that it was nice to see the justice system working smoothly for a change – though of course it had taken long months and a lot of effort to get the restraining order and the initial charge in the first place.

I also attended training about honour-based violence. If you're not familiar with the term, the official definition from the CPS at time of writing is:

"an incident or crime involving violence, threats of violence, intimidation coercion or abuse (including psychological, physical, sexual, financial or emotional abuse) which has or may have been committed to protect or defend the honour of an individual, family and/or community for alleged or perceived breaches of the family and/or community's code of behaviour."

In layman's terms, it's abuse or even murders that are carried out by the victim's family, partner, or members of their community, to defend the family or community's perceived 'honour' or in response to an individual's attempt to break away from the constraints their family or community have imposed on them. Incidents that can trigger honour-based abuse can include adultery, divorce, refusing to enter an arranged marriage, or being homosexual – among other things. You'll not be surprised to learn that most victims are girls, and most perpetrators men, though both men and women can be victims and suspects of honour-based abuse.

I never worked on any honour-based abuse cases during my time in TVP, but the training was recommended for everyone by our inspector. There have been high-profile cases where the police mishandled honour-based abuse and people died, so it was an important topic. A few things I learned that you might find useful:

- It's inadvisable to share missing person posts on social media unless they've been posted by an official and established missing persons charity, the police, or similar. This is because, if a victim does escape and move to a different location, the community or family will often do everything they can to try and find the person. They might report the person as missing or a hire private investigator to find them; sharing a private person's missing person post might inadvertently help the community find the victim and take their revenge on them to restore their 'honour'.
- Police officers specifically were warned to be careful when using interpreters. They can often be from the same community as the victim, and pass information on to the community or family that might lead to further abuse.

During my first three months in DAIU I also had my first ever rape case where I was OIC – the one I mentioned during my CID course. As I said, I initially protested that I hadn't had the specialist training to be an OIC for a rape case – but I was told that there was nobody with the training who could take it on, so someone had to.

The interview with the suspect was interesting because he and his lawyer seemed to be at loggerheads. He gave a 'no comment' interview, but frequently asked for breaks to speak to his lawyer. I was conducting the interview with a colleague, and it seemed plain to me that the suspect wanted to talk to us, but that his lawyer kept telling him it wasn't in his best interests – every time they came back from their discussions, he would continue replying "no comment".

We had all the evidence, and were about to send it off to CPS to get a charging decision, when the victim withdrew her support for the case; on that basis, we decided to drop it, too.

Finally, I remember taking part in a PolSA search after a celebrity jewel theft. A PolSA, or Police Search Adviser, is an officer who has been specially trained to conduct search operations for a range of incidents, including counter-terrorism, crime, and missing person searches. Basically, these officers are really good at searching for stuff – but don't ask them to look for your keys, because they might start ripping up your floorboards. My sergeant said it would be good experience for me, so off I went.

We were searching a studio apartment, and the thoroughness of the search was staggering. There were five of us on the search, and it still took us about four hours. Each room was divided into quadrants, furniture was moved and searched. In the wardrobe, every item of clothing had to be felt by hand to check whether anything had been sewn into it. We didn't find the item, in the end, but it was still fascinating – and of course it was exciting to be involved in a high-profile crime involving a celebrity.

So I found myself getting to grips with the daily life in DAIU. Some promising jobs, some disappointing, some infuriating. In that sense, it was just like the rest of my time in the police. I hoped that my relative level of experience compared to my time in ICR, PCT and CID, and the nature of the cases I was dealing with, would make things more satisfying for me.

CHAPTER 34

ATTEMPTED MURDER

"Come on, Alicia," my colleague Brenda muttered under her breath.

We were standing at the bottom of a block of low flats in the chilly winter morning air. I was now three months into my time at DAIU, and on this day I was helping Brenda take the victim of an attempt murder, who we'll call Alicia, to Crown court. Alicia had been withdrawn and anxious for a while, and barely engaged with police anymore. The attempted murder happened over a year ago and she really didn't want to attend court after all this time. She'd told us before that she hoped they would just let it go by now.

I really understood her. The crime itself had been very traumatic, and then Alicia had been through the whole police process. The interview, the forms, the victim impact statement, the updates about the case. Every contact with us brought the trauma back to the front of her mind. After more than a year, I'd have quite liked to move on from the whole incident if I was in her position, too. Instead, she had the prospect of cross-examination on the stand looming over her, as well as facing the man who had tried to murder her.

After about 10 minutes, though, Alicia finally appeared. She'd done her make up, and was well groomed. But her anguish was plain to see on her face.

We exchanged some pleasantries and got in the car. On the journey, we tried to make some small talk in the car, as police officers always do, but Alicia didn't really respond. Brenda stopped at a petrol station on the way and asked me to fill up while she talked to Alicia. I could tell that she wanted to try and reassure Alicia without me there – after all, Alicia didn't know me.

"Don't fill the car up with Diesel!" Brenda shouted to me as I moved round to the pump. She might not have been feeling like Alicia, but it was obvious that Brenda was on edge as well. She'd been leading this case for a long time and wanted to get justice.

"I wasn't planning on it!" I shouted back. Oddly, the tension in the car wasn't really affecting me. Probably because I was tagging along as a driver, really – the stakes were pretty low for me.

Once we arrived at court, we parked in a large parking lot where police can park for free. We walked across to Reading Crown court, across Forbury gardens. Not long before, these gardens had been the site of a terrorist attack. Three people had been killed and three more injured in a horrendous stabbing attack. An off-duty officer had actually followed the terrorist while speaking to police on the phone.

We let Alicia enter through the victim's entrance (which ensures the suspect and victim do not cross each other in the hallways). Brenda and I went in through the main entrance and into the courtroom. Brenda spoke with the barrister for a bit to make sure everything was ready to go. Not long after that, the judge entered the room and everything went very formal and traditional. Just like you see in the movies, everyone has to stand up when the judge enters or exits the room. When the judge is in the room, only the barristers will speak, using formal (and I would say haughty) language – except when hearing from witnesses, the defendant and the accused. Much of the talks, debates and decisions are made without the jury present. It's all about deciding how or if something will be presented to the jury, to try and avoid biasing the jury.

At the beginning of the hearing, we saw some body-worn video footage from the police who attended the incident. In the footage, the suspect was agitated and holding a large kitchen knife. He refused to put it down and police negotiated with him for twenty minutes before he finally surrendered the knife. We watched the whole twenty minutes of footage.

Next, a firearms officer who attended the scene was called into the witness box. There was some confusion about what he did with the knife once the defendant handed it to him. The defence barrister tried to exploit this to make the firearms officer look incompetent or inconsistent. However, it didn't really fly. The officer gave short and brief answers and looked confident and competent.

Next, it was Alicia's turn in the witness box.

She had requested a screen that ensures the suspect cannot see the victim. It's one of the 'special measures' that victims of crime can request (another is giving evidence via a video link). I remembered how much these special measures had been described and lauded by our trainers at Sully; in real life, I couldn't get around the fact that this screen was a piece of plastic on wheels. The suspect had to go and sit in the far left of their box because otherwise they would still have been able to see the victim. If they really wanted to be difficult or intimidating, they could do so without even having to leave their box – though the jury wouldn't have looked favourably on that, I imagine. Still, the special measures felt measurably less special to me.

With the screen in place, Alicia gave her evidence – and then came the cross-examination. I remembered my own experience of cross-examination from the CID course just a few months ago. I found it horrible, and I hadn't even been the victim of a real crime – let alone one as traumatising as Alicia had. She was extremely brave.

Alicia did incredibly well. I couldn't see her behind the screen, but I could hear her speak – she sounded clear and confident. For twenty minutes, the barrister tried to put words in her mouth, but she didn't let him. Her answers were short, to the point, and consistent.

Finally, Alicia left the box. I'd agreed with Brenda that I would escort her home while Brenda stayed for the rest of the trial. Alicia was incredibly relieved.

"I can finally breathe," she said to me.

I was so impressed at her bravery and her composure; I told her that she'd done incredibly well. We left the court building as quickly as we could and I drove Alica home. She was much chattier; a very obvious weight had been lifted from her shoulders.

Once we were back at Alicia's house, I looked down at my phone. I had about ten missed calls from Brenda. I called her back.

"Where have you been?" She asked.

"Sorry, I was driving and talking to Alicia. My phone was still on silent from the court room."

"Did everything go OK? Did Alicia get home alright?"

"Yes, we're here now. Why, what's up?"

"About two minutes after Alicia gave evidence the judge called for a break in proceedings, and the defendant was allowed to leave the room. I was trying to tell you so you could make sure that they didn't cross paths in the hallway."

"Oh my god, really?" I asked, shocked. "That's insane. Thankfully we didn't encounter him. Just a normal drive home."

"Phew," Brenda exhaled. "Thanks for your help."

I was extremely relieved that we'd not added to Alicia's trauma by having her attacker bump into her just after she'd given evidence against him. But I was also shocked at the criminal justice system. How could they treat victims this way? We'd just dragged this poor woman to court to be brutally cross examined, and then the judge had allowed the person who attempted to kill her to roam the hallways of the court as she was trying to leave. Having spent the morning with the victim, I could picture all too clearly what the impact of that meeting would have been. The trauma it would bring back for her, the fear, the sense of vulnerability. I was left feeling more disillusioned than ever by this system.

Since we're talking about the justice system, I should mention at this point that my Wexham Park assault case, which I had been so determined to see through to the end, was all but dead in the water. There was still no movement, and it had been getting so awkward giving meaningless updates to the victims that I just stopped. By the time I left the police, the case still hadn't gone to trial.

CHAPTER 35

CLARE'S LAW

As my work in DAIU continued, I found once again that I had better results with my victims when I went beyond the bureaucracy of the RMO. There's one chain of events from that time that stuck with me – though as with everything I experienced at the police, good results were often followed by bad ones.

I'd just achieved a conviction at court – assault and coercive control – after a successful investigation. The victim and I had spent months building a relationship during the case, which had been graded as high-risk. After the sentencing, however, the case was re-graded as medium risk. I liked this as it meant I wouldn't be forced by an RMO to call her every month. Instead, I could just decide when to contact her, based on my own judgement.

Most officers in my position would have dropped the contact completely and moved on to other work – but I was a bit worried about how the victim would manage the transition from a lot of intense contact to almost none. I also knew that her partner had received a suspended sentence, and I wanted to keep in touch with her to make sure he didn't cause her any further trouble.

Just quickly – if you've read that term before and never really understood what it means, a suspended sentence means you don't go to prison.

When I called, the victim seemed grateful to hear from me and told me she was starting to recover from the abuse and the pressures of the court case, and that she was getting the right support. She also told me that she heard her ex-partner was now dating another woman; let's call her Hailey.

This was valuable information – another reason to feel pleased that I'd taken the initiative and time to call her. I decided to use this information to submit a Clare's Law request on behalf of Hailey.

Clare's Law, officially known in England as the Domestic Violence Disclosure Scheme, is a policy (oddly enough it's not actually a formal law in the UK, despite its name) named for Clare Wood, who in 2009 was murdered by her ex-boyfriend – a man who had a violent history that was known to the police, but not to Clare. It gives a person's partner, a 'right to ask' for information about a person's history. It also gives people a 'right to know', which allows the police to disclose information about a person if they feel they are at risk. It's an extremely useful tool for officers, as it gives you the chance to prevent abuse from happening by informing people of their partner's abusive past.

This was the first time I'd submitted a Clare's Law application and of course there were many bureaucratic hoops to jump through. But I was excited – the chance to proactively prevent someone becoming a victim of abuse doesn't come around very often in the police. Most of the time, we just react to crimes after they've happened.

I created a record on Niche and asked my sergeant what should happen next. He confirmed to me that another department had the responsibility of reviewing these requests. They would gather more information and decide if a disclosure was appropriate – but if they approved the disclosure, it would frequently be done by DAIU. So I might have had the chance to actually deliver the disclosure myself.

In the meantime, I had a child protection conference to attend in relation to this case. Similar to a MARAC meeting or a Strat meeting, a child protection conference was another meeting of different bodies to pool intelligence and decide what the best course of action to take was for any children in a case – in this instance, the woman's two teenage children. This one was organised by social services, though.

A key component of child protection conferences was that we all had to take a vote on whether we believed the children were at risk of significant harm or not. If we voted that they were, then social services would stay involved with the family. That didn't necessarily mean the children would be taken away or anything – it just meant that social services would do more assessments and offer whatever support was needed.

Needless to say, I took the vote very seriously and I asked my tutor Brian what I should consider. Brian was a kind, diligent and good officer, which is why his response has stayed with me ever since:

"Oh yeah," he said, "usually you just get a feel for the room and go along with what other people say."

I was flabbergasted. How could that be his position?! This was a serious part of our job, and another opportunity to prevent harm or crime. Momentarily at a loss for words, I finally came back with:

"What if they come to me first?"

"Well, you'll just have to improvise," he shrugged.

Needless to say, I did not improvise. I gave the matter due thought and consideration, and I voted for social services staying involved – after all, the offender's sentence was suspended so he wasn't completely out of the picture. Staying involved won the vote in the end – though now I can't be sure how many people believed that was right and how many were taking Brian's approach and going with what I said.

Anyway, about a month after submitting the Clare's Law request, I decided to check whether the report had been dealt with. It was possible that it was still caught up in the bureaucracy of the police, but whenever I thought about it I felt uneasy knowing this perpetrator was potentially abusing or trapping another woman while we knew about his past.

I opened the record. Disclosure hadn't been approved, or even refused. The record had been closed because the woman, apparently, was not contactable.

I was perplexed. Within ten minutes I was able to find a potential address and phone number on our internal system, as well as the school her children went to. Unless she was avoiding the police, there's no way it was impossible to contact her. I shared my concern with my sergeant at his desk.

"Don't worry about it," he told me bluntly. "Not your responsibility." His eyes slid back to his screen again.

"But it is my responsibility," I pressed. "I am a police officer. Please, I need to make sure this has been followed up on. It would give me peace of mind."

The sergeant reassured me that the matter had been followed up with and that everyone had done their duty. He was kind about it, but it was clear that he wasn't going to help me make a difference here.

I emailed the department that dealt with the case, shared my concerns, and provided possible solutions. They took ages to send me a generic reply saying they weren't going to do anything.

A month or so later, Hailey made a report to police about controlling behaviour by her partner. I can't remember the details of the report, and my team didn't deal with the case – I just saw the name pop up on Niche. But the disappointment, disillusionment, and desolation I felt in that moment will stay in my memory for a long time. We'd had all the tools to prevent this. The information was there, the policy was there, and I was there, trying to make it all work. But the police bureaucracy had said no – and now this woman was enduring potential abuse, and I had been unable to do anything about it.

CHAPTER 36

BB GUN

During my time in DAIU, I had my third – and final, as it turned out – meeting with my portfolio assessor, James. You might remember that as part of my course, I had to gather a portfolio of different types of crimes and incidents that I'd dealt with. It was why I went for those two shifts with the traffic team back in CID.

Those meetings were always a bit funny. James was a nice enough man, and kind enough in his way. But he did like to talk at me a lot, generally about various procedures and details about the portfolio. He would often tell me how silly things were, or that things would be completely fine – I'm not sure he ever realised that those things made me feel more nervous than before. He also never asked me how I was getting on in any sort of pastoral sense. I got the sense that it just never occurred to him to ask.

As the end of the DC DHEP programme was approaching, James and I were starting to think more seriously about how to tick off various elements of my portfolio that I would struggle to do in DAIU. The portfolio was designed for uniform officers, not detectives, so it wasn't easy to get everything signed off.

"We still need to tick off 'conflict'," said James.

This was frustrating – I'd dealt with conflict in ICR. There was my Wexham park assault suspect, of course, and the man I'd guarded on a bed watch and had restrained initially, which would have counted as physical conflict. There was also a rather funny incident with a guy who was in a pub and got very irrational and aggressive. We arrested him, and he resisted – so he was restrained. Once he was in the van, he started smashing his head against the door repeatedly and had to be restrained again. Soon after, though, his rage subsided and he became very sad and morose; I ended up comforting the man even though he'd been behaving in an extremely hostile manner towards me not five minutes earlier. Then he fell asleep with his head in my lap. Soon after, he woke up and was angry again. By the time we got to the custody desk he was in a great mood. We suspected he was under the influence of some substance, so extreme were his mood swings. The funniest part for me, though, was that the tracksuit he was given in custody had no pockets. Yet over and over again, he kept rubbing his hands down his legs, trying to put his hands in non-existent pockets. For some reason, it just gave me the giggles.

But I digress. Even though I'd dealt with quite a few incidents which could have been described as 'conflict' while in ICR, they didn't count towards the portfolio. In an absurd twist that won't surprise you by this stage, the incidents we attended during our ten weeks on ICR counted towards a separate portfolio, and couldn't be used twice.

So, James proposed to book in a few extra uniform shifts on Friday and Saturday nights to try and tick the boxes. To say I was apprehensive would be an understatement. My last two uniforms shifts, with the road traffic unit, had left me a nervous wreck; since then, my mind had only become more fragile. I was in a relatively good place at this point in DAIU – the welcoming team, and focus on victims (despite the bureaucracy) was helping. But I could feel how fragile that peace was. I was still pushing things down and blocking them out like I was in CID; it wouldn't take much to bring me down.

I kept telling myself 'these are the last shifts you'll ever do in ICR. You just have to get through them and then you're out of there.' My sergeant helped enormously – he told me that even if I didn't get the boxes ticked off, I wouldn't have to go back; he was prepared to take it up the chain of command, if necessary.

"You're part of this team now," he said.

So, with trepidation in my heart, I soon found myself back in a uniform squad briefing room. I was doing these shifts in Maidenhead, with a different team with officers I'd never met before, and thankfully I knew what to expect.

As usual, I was paired with a more experienced officer. You always end up making a lot of small talk during the shift while driving around in the patrol car. My crewmate, who we'll call Dave, was kind and understanding of the fact I didn't have much experience in uniform. Most importantly, he was willing to explain things.

He seemed to have the standard attitude you often encountered in officers: past defeat and now resigned to the shitty reality of the job. Unwilling to leave because of the stability and pension, and perhaps not knowing what other jobs they could do, but completely dispassionate about the job.

"I would honestly not recommend this job to anyone" he said at one point.

I was never quite sure whether he meant it or not. Complaining was the status quo in the police and sometimes I wasn't sure whether people were just following the crowd, or whether they had really accepted that they were going to do a job for years on end that they were uninspired and not passionate about. With his helpful demeanour, I hope that Dave was the former.

Soon, control asked us to attend a nearby park. A passerby had seen a child in possession of a BB gun, waving it around and pointing it at people. We arrived and quickly spotted the child, a ten-year-old, who fitted the description. About ten other children were standing around him laughing; when they saw us coming, their eyes all got a bit wide as they realised what was about to unfold.

"Do you know why we're here?" Dave said sternly to the boy.

"I don't know, but maybe because of this…" he took out a small metal BB gun from his sweater pocket.

"Give that to me," Dave ordered him; the child promptly surrendered the gun. As Dave put it away in a pocket, I wondered if the gun needed to first be made safe by ARV as per procedure. Did you have to do that for BB guns? In any case, I dropped the thought – it seemed impossible not to first put the gun away in a pocket somewhere.

My colleague and I explained to the boy that what he was doing was a crime. He said he didn't know and was just playing with it. Apparently, his brother gave it to him. When it became apparent that he didn't understand the gravity of the situation, Dave decided to bring out the big guns.

"We're taking you home to speak to your mum," he announced.

That did it. The boy burst into tears.

"NO, NO, I'M NOT GOING!" he screamed. And so saying, he crouched down on the floor, face in his hands. Dave did his best to encourage him out of this position with a few 'C'mon now's, but the child didn't budge; he just kept sobbing away, face in hands.

I realised that a stern approach was probably not going to work, and if we kept it up we'd have to manhandle him into the car – not great. I crouched down next to him and put my hand on his shoulder.

"It's alright, you're not going to be arrested," I told him in my best motherly tone.

"I didn't know it was illegal!" he sniffed through his tears.

"Well, now you do," I said. "Sometimes you have to learn these things like this."

After a little bit more encouragement like this he finally stood up and walked to our car. I made sure to praise him for it.

As we drove to his house, we ran a few checks on the address and I wondered what kind of house and family he would belong to. There were some occurrences linked to the address – possibly his brother or cousin, from the notes. But when we got there, nothing seemed too amiss. The only real issue was that when we spoke to the mother, she seemed to think the whole thing was a bit exaggerated.

"He's just playing," she said to us, a slight tone of disbelief in her voice.

"Yes, but with a BB gun," I stressed. "These are not toys."

In case you're on her side of the argument, even lower-powered BB guns can cause serious damage to a person – especially if a pellet accidentally goes in someone's eyes.

We gave the mother some words of advice about not letting her son use items like this anymore, and I would have liked to leave it at that. However, Dave said that procedure dictated we give the boy a 'community resolution'. A community resolution, or CR, is essentially an official record which states that an informal resolution was reached regarding an incident. Once again, the police had found a way to formalise an informal process.

Of course, that meant more paperwork for me and Dave – someone cannot receive a CR for the same offence twice, so we needed a record of it. Dave brought several pieces of paper in from the car which contained the CR template. It was even more bureaucratic than I had realised. I barely understood the instructions myself as I read through them; they were full of legal jargon.

"This is the part you have to read out loud to the suspect," Dave said. There was half an A4 of text which had to be read verbatim. I also had to switch on my body cam so there was proof that I'd read it to the boy.

So, armed with my paperwork, I called the boy in to where I was sat in the living room and I explained in simple terms first what we were going to do. That was OK, but then I had to read out this piece of text:

You are suspected of (give details of offence, and reasons for that suspicion). You have the right to be informed of these details. At this stage it is proposed that the matter be dealt with informally and I will provide you with an opportunity to make recompense for your actions. This is voluntary and if you agree and complete the process you will not normally be subject to any further police investigation. Failure to complete the agreed actions may result in the matter being formally investigated and you being liable to prosecution. This declaration would then be presented as part of the case against you.

And then, once we've agreed on the recommendations and those have been signed by the appropriate adult, I had to read this bit out:

*Community Resolutions are not recorded on the Police National Computer; however the information will be held by local police. (Where the offence relates to a notifiable crime the offender must be informed that a crime has been recorded and they will be held as responsible for it.) This information will not be made available as a result of a standard Disclosure and Barring Service *DBS) check, but may be disclosed if an application for an enhanced DBS check is made (previously CRB check).*

Do you understand what that means?

In other words, it was completely impossible for a ten-year-old boy to understand. I felt absurd reciting all this stuff to him as he sat sobbing in front of me. I decided that I needed to try and translate it into something he would understand before we left.

"This all sounds quite complicated, but it just means we're giving you a warning, nothing more," I said.

Up until the CR, it felt like we had dealt well with the incident and I had felt like a proper officer doing good work. After the CR, I just felt a bit ridiculous – and somewhat incredulous. Was it really necessary to do all this paperwork? Couldn't we just have said 'don't do it again' and made a full record of the incident on our systems when we returned to the station?

Ironically, in the end that BB gun incident didn't count as conflict – and the rest of the shift passed relatively uneventfully. My second shift was spent entirely on a cell watch – remember the story from earlier about the suspect who liked dirty protests? That was my last ever shift on ICR.

True to his word, my sergeant didn't let me go back on ICR after that. We found something from my past that we could use to tick conflict off my portfolio, and that was that.

CHAPTER 37

NRPF

A few times at DAIU, our team dealt with victims who were NRPF. This stands for 'no recourse to public funds'. It means that a person, for whatever reason, has no access to UK publicly funded services – mainly various benefits. The vast majority of people with NRPF are migrants from outside the European Economic Area who are either undocumented, awaiting an appeal on their immigration status, or who are being sponsored by someone else. That includes migrants who are in the UK on a spousal visa – which is where their worlds and ours often collided.

When domestic abuse is involved, the complications caused by NRPF status can be devastating. Imagine if you were being abused – but your abuser was your only source of any kind of support. If you left them, you'd be unable to access benefits, and essentially have no status in the UK. There are technically legal routes for victims of DA in this position to get some form of status – and therefore access to benefits and support – but as with any procedure involving immigration, it takes time. So where do victims go in the meantime? In my experience, nowhere good.

I arrived in the office for the start of a late shift (so at 14:00) to hear that there was a family waiting in the reception at Slough police station: a mother and two kids. They'd fled a violent partner in the UK but were NRPF. I asked my team what the plan was in these kinds of situations. The answers were all very much focused on the usual police procedures:

"We'll do a Dash risk assessment."

"We'll ask the victim if she wants to provide a statement."

"We need to check if she'll want special measures at court."

All of which was fine, of course – but my mind was dwelling much more on how we were going to make sure this family had safe temporary housing. I'm willing to bet that the victim was similarly much more interested in these questions than in her DA case. And to make matters worse, in my experience women's refuges generally did not accept referrals who were NRPF.

As soon as we got our admin done, the family was told to wait. And to my relief, at around 8pm that evening a hotel was booked for them. I drove over to Slough with a colleague to escort the woman and her kids to the hotel and check them in; on the way I called and asked her to meet us in the parking lot of the police station.

When we arrived, I saw an Indian woman with two kids, probably about six or seven years old if I had to guess. She thanked me for bringing her to the hotel, and told me how she'd spent the whole day waiting around in the police station, uncertain of what was going to happen.

"Have you eaten?" I asked her.

"We got a meal at the Sikh temple," she told me. In case you didn't know, gurdwaras (the proper name for Sikh temples) operate community kitchens called Langars, run by volunteers, that serve meals to anyone who asks for one. I remember being absolutely baffled the first time I heard a homeless man casually tell me he'd eaten at the temple earlier that day, before I was familiar with the practice.

"How long can we stay here?" The woman asked me.

"The hotel is booked for one night," I told her, "but unfortunately I can't tell you what will happen after that." My heart broke slightly as I said it. I felt so sad seeing the family in this situation: homeless, with no clue where to go and no money, and all the trauma of domestic abuse on their heads too. But I was glad that at least I could offer them a hotel for a night, and tried to sustain myself with that thought.

The next day, another family in a very similar situation showed up. My sergeant briefed the team at around 3pm and said that Children's Social Care (CSC) should be providing accommodation for both families. When there are kids involved, regardless of NRPF status, CSC have a duty of care to provide accommodation so that the children are not street homeless. Unfortunately, a single adult would likely be left homeless if they can't find a shelter that will accept NRPF people, but these are rare.

Just before 10pm, the office phone rang. I picked it up; it was the mother. The police reception had closed earlier that evening and since then they'd just been sitting on the curb in front of a closed police station, waiting for a phone call from CSC. The call had not come.

"Just give me a moment, and I'll see what's going on," I told them. I put them on hold and turned to my sergeant. "It's the family from today. They're on the street. CSC hasn't called. Shall we get them a hotel?"

"No," my sergeant replied. "This is CSC's job, not ours. The police do not have funds for this."

"But… what if CSC never call?" I asked. I'd dealt with CSC and housing offices before, and though they are good people doing their best I would never trust any word or promise they gave.

"Not our job," my sergeant replied. "Shut down your laptop. It's time to go home."

I reluctantly shut down my laptop, feeling numb. How could I go home and sleep, knowing that one family – and, let's face it, probably two – with kids were on the street? I was extremely sceptical that CSC would call and sort them shelter tonight.

I considered paying for the hotel myself. But if I paid today, then what about tomorrow and the day after? Would social services see this as confirmation that in fact the police or a third party were taking care of the situation and there was no need for them to intervene? It felt like just the kind of thing that would happen. And then I felt a surge of disgust that the system made me, a police officer, think twice about helping out a family in such desperate need.

I'd felt bad before while driving home from work, but that was probably the worst. Most days I felt like I'd not had the chance to help anyone who really needed it; on this day, I'd had the opportunity to help someone in dire need of assistance and not done anything. In fact, I was told not to do anything by my sergeant, and it disconcerted me how lightly he and my other colleagues had taken the situation. My sergeant wasn't the only one to say, 'not our job', brush the whole thing off and go home at the end of the shift.

Was that what years of police work does to people? You need thick skin to be in the police – if you let every case get you down, you'd be sobbing into your boots by lunchtime. But being so walled off that not even an opportunity to make a difference to a vulnerable woman and two small children could motivate my team to take action, was awful. My team, the domestic abuse specialists, weren't prepared to help.

You might be reading this thinking that they were right. It wasn't our job; it was the responsibility of CSC to house these families. But to me, in that moment, it felt like an absolute cop-out. Who is supposed to be the absolute last line of defence against situations like this? In my mind, it was us – the police. And we'd just spent all day dealing with their case. So it wasn't even like this was some story happening far away from us that we were hearing about. My team actively chose to down tools and stop helping this family.

I thought about the way all of us were enticed – that's what it felt like, by this point – into applying for the police. Promises of making a difference and helping the most vulnerable in society. Driving home in the dark, that felt like a big fat fucking lie. We cared about ticking our boxes, getting our risk assessments and statements done, and a wealth of other paperwork. We hoped that the rat's nest of paper might eventually help the victims we spoke to, but as long as it protected us from being blamed or reprimanded for something, that was enough. And when it came to really, truly making a difference? We tossed it away.

I never found out what happened to either family. Honestly, I was too afraid to look up their records; I just couldn't imagine there was a good outcome for either of them.

CHAPTER 38

I QUIT

The month after that night was my lowest at TVP. I felt exhausted all the time, and I noticed I was growing more cynical as my disillusionment with the police began to take hold. I dreaded every shift; once I was there, it was about ten minutes before I started watching the clock, counting down the hours until I could leave. I could no longer hide from the thought that had been lurking in my unconscious mind since CID: I needed to quit. For nearly two years I'd clung to the dream of being a detective, but now it was time to look it square in the face.

I hated being a detective. I wanted out.

Honestly, the only reason I was still staying by this point was for the qualifications. At the end of the two-year probation, DC DHEP graduates like me would get a Diploma in Professional Policing Practice from university, and my Professionalising Investigations Programme level 2 qualification (known as PIP2 for short). I'd put a load of work into earning those qualifications; alongside all of the shit from work, I'd still been doing university assignments. I asked a few times about when I would be assessed for my PIP2, but I kept being told to be patient.

"Don't worry, I know you want your PIP2 done so you can be on your way to the Met," my sergeant said cheerfully to me at one point. What made him believe I wanted to stay in policing for a second longer than I had to, I have no idea. But I let the lie sit there – it was easier than telling him I was utterly burnt out and ready to quit.

So, I hung in there, hating the work and feeling awful.

Meanwhile my PIP2 was delayed until further notice. I asked why I couldn't be assessed for it. I was told that there was a backlog due to a lack of assessors available, and that they had to prioritise other officers who had been waiting longer than me.

I didn't quite believe them; I knew that other people in my DC DHEP class had been assessed and got their PIP2, but not me.

"Don't worry about it," they told me, "it's not that important."

It plainly wasn't that important to them, but it was to me – it represented a lot of the hard work, suffering, and effort of the last two years.

Then, one day, I was called in by the sergeant.

"Jade, do you have a moment to talk? It's nothing to worry about."

Nobody has ever said 'it's nothing to worry about' and then given good news.

I went in and sat down in front of the sergeant.

"It's really nothing to worry about," he told me evenly, "but I have to give you a reg 13 informal."

I was stunned. Regulation 13 is the process that kicks into action when a student officer isn't performing to the expected standard. The focus is on helping the officer improve their performance, but if they don't meet the required standards, then it could become a formal HR process which in the worst-case scenario could escalate to the officer getting dismissed. The "informal" is the first stage of the process, where a plan is put together.

"Can you tell me why I'm being given this?" I asked him.

"Well," he said, "I'm really just passing it on. It's connected to you failing one of your university assignments, apparently."

That didn't make any sense to me. I'd failed assignments before, and they hadn't resulted in a reg 13. I'd just had to resubmit my work for the module.

"Do you support this?" I asked my sergeant. "Have I been underperforming in my work here?"

"No, not at all," he replied quickly, "you're doing a good job. I expect this has come from the university coordinator." He pushed a piece of paper towards me. "Can you sign this please, to show that you've accepted it?"

A wave of anger oozed up through my stomach.

"No," I told him flatly." I don't agree with it, and you don't agree with it, and university hasn't said anything to me about this before now. I'm sorry but I'm not signing it."

"I completely understand that," the sergeant said, and we were done.

I left the office upset and angry, and pretty much immediately started writing an email to the university coordinator. The email was straight to the point. No pleasantries. I wanted an explanation for the reg 13 which hit me out of nowhere. But if I was angry when I sent it, the response sent me into a fury. The coordinator sent me some bland nonsense: "it's nothing to worry about, it's just a way to support you," and so on. How typical of the police to create a disciplinary procedure and call it 'a way to support you'. It felt more to me like I was being pushed out with some nonsensical bit of bureaucracy. I typed back:

"If you want to support me, pick up the phone and ask me what I need. Don't serve me with a reg 13."

I got a reply from my old trainer Amber, who was also a course coordinator on the police side (there were two coordinators, one from the uni and one from TVP), telling me she was disappointed with how rude I'd been, but I really didn't care. I ended up having to take another two days off with stress, and while I was at home, everything came crashing in on me. All the difficulties of the past two years, all the disillusionment with the job, all the hard decisions, all the bureaucracy that got in the way of doing the job.

The reality was all the reasons why I had joined had either become irrelevant or been revealed as not true. I didn't feel like I was making a difference, or that I could go above and beyond for people. I didn't like investigating cases, which was just a conveyor-belt process of complex and technical admin, which half the time we knew full well would never get a charge or conviction. It all felt utterly meaningless. I was a cog in a broken system, meat for the bureaucratic grinder. Only those with an attitude of 'I get my salary at the end of the month and I get a nice pension' stayed in this job. The dreamers and idealists did not survive long. My dream job had boiled down to a breakdown, burnout, and a disciplinary procedure due to a failed university assignment.

I was done. Qualifications or not, it was time to go.

I didn't tell anyone how I was feeling at first, but they all guessed something was up. Mainly because I took all of my remaining annual leave in one go. Once I got back from that, I was doing some work with one of my colleagues when they turned to me.

"Are you OK? You look like you don't want to come into work."

And in that moment, I couldn't lie to her. So I told her exactly how I was feeling. She was kind and sympathetic, and – thank God – didn't try to convince me to stay.

"Go and speak to the sergeant," she told me.

By now we actually had a new sergeant, and from our meeting it was pretty plain that he didn't know how to handle the situation.

"Well, send your resignation to this email address, I guess," was all he really said on the matter.

So I sent in my email, and that was that. I had officially resigned from the police.

CHAPTER 39

LAST CASES: FISHER HAT AND DEMENTIA

Once I'd finally made the leap to quit, I felt like a burden had been lifted off my shoulders. Instead of an infinite number of soul-crushing and mind-numbing shifts I now had a short and finite number of shifts left, and I could start counting down.

At that point, only the sergeant and the officer who I'd spoken to before speaking to the sergeant knew that I'd quit. Which, of course, meant that within a few days the TVP gossip machine had spread the news to every corner of Slough police station and the Windsor DAIU office. I got an email out of the blue from an old colleague in CID asking me about it a few days after I resigned. I also got a call from Amber, asking me if there was anything they could do to make me stay. I appreciated the thought, but it really was too little, too late. My mind was made up.

My sister was happy for me.

"I'm so glad to hear you say that," she told me. "I've been really worried about you. These last few months you've seemed like a different person. If you push past your limits any further, you may suffer the consequences for a long time."

I had resigned, but I still needed to work my notice. In fact, during my notice period I officially passed my probation – a slightly strange turn of events. Nevertheless, I decided to make the most of my last month as a police officer.

The last month of my service was actually an interesting one. A high-risk and prolific offender had been released from prison and immediately started stalking and harassing his ex-partner – who we'll call Lillian – again. Besides being a DA offender (and so well-known to my team), he was also a drug dealer and was involved in various types of crimes. He was one of those people that when you open their file there is a long, long list of 'occurrences' there. In this latest occurrence, the offender had visited his ex-partner's address twice in a short timespan. One time he had smashed a window, and the other time pressed his buttocks up against a window. Both times, his ex-partner called the police – but when they arrived, he was already gone.

The offender's name, I noticed, was Rahul – and a shock of recognition went through me.

You've already met him. He was my bed watch suspect who had almost been tasered and faked heart attack symptoms.

The ex-partner lived alone with three young children. My sergeant convinced her to go to a nearby hotel for a few nights to ensure her safety (paid for by police this time). She accepted, and I went to pick them up and take them to the hotel. She was keen to make some small talk, but I wasn't very talkative – with three kids in the back, I was being extra careful to focus on the road. After a few days in the hotel however, she decided to go back home as it was easier to bring the kids to school from there.

A few days later, Rahul struck again. Lillian called 999. My team was in the office at the time; we gathered round the radio to follow along as the incident unfolded. We heard the control room relaying the job and the information to the teams on duty in the local area. However, even though this was a grade 1 job, there were no available units to assist.

After a few seconds my sergeant sprung.

"Get your kit. We're going," he said to the team.

It must have taken us about 30 minutes from that point to actually get to the victim's address. Although the offender had left, I approved of my sergeant's proactive attitude. As an investigative unit, we rarely deployed – it felt good to be doing something to make a difference.

Lillian said that Rahul kept calling her, and had called her three hundred times in the last few hours. She expected that he was drugged up and still somewhere in the area. We agreed; he kept telling her on the phone that he could "pick her up somewhere".

Lillian told us that she was considering meeting Rahul to try and bring an end to the crazy harassment. Of course, none of us agreed that this was a good idea and we advised Lillian to stay put. Me, my sergeant, and the rest of the DAIU team kept 'area searching' around her house (in case you're not sure, 'area searching' is police lingo for 'searching the area'). All the while, Rahul kept calling Lillian's phone. At one point he texted her:

"Why are those pigs at your house?!"

If he was close enough to see that we were in the house, he was close enough to arrest, if we could catch him.

I felt a rush of adrenaline. Surely, I could find him. If I could, it would be a nice last arrest to make. It might even involve a bit of a chase, something I'd wanted to do but had never had the opportunity. So I continued the search, fear and excitement jostling for position in my head. After a foot search didn't turn anything up, we got in the car. But it was a bust. There was no trace of him. After about an hour we called off the search. We were disappointed but committed to trying again. Rahul was taking up all of DAIU's resources, and his behaviour was escalating dangerously. We had to trace and arrest him soon.

The next day, Lillian called 999 again. She was driving and had just passed a black Range Rover. She told the police that she was certain she'd seen Rahul driving the car, wearing a fisher's hat. She gave us the plate, and the game was on.

Anticipation hovered in the air in the office. Behind closed doors, higher ranking officers were making plans which were very hush-hush and not shared with the rank and file – probably some sort of covert operation. Everyone had their radios on, listening for an update.

Around three hours later, it happened. An unmarked road traffic unit spotted the vehicle and passed his location to control over the radio. The unit started following the car and was connecting with other road traffic colleagues to put down a stinger.

Everyone in the office had dropped what they were doing and was listening with excitement to the radio. After a little while, the action began.

"Stinger deployed."

"Vehicle making off! In pursuit." Everyone crept closer to the edge of their seat. Making off with tyres shredded by a stinger meant Rahul would barely be able to control the vehicle. This could not go right for long.

"Left, left on Brackenbury Lane."

"Contact made!"

Everyone gasped. That meant the car in pursuit had rammed the Ranger Rover to bring him to a stop.

"Suspect making off on foot! In pursuit!"

"C'mon get him!" Everyone started shouting at the radio. There was silence for a while. The tension was palpable.

Eventually:

"Male in cuffs."

Everyone in the office cheered and clapped. I got the sense that none of them had seen that much excitement in a long time. I certainly hadn't, and I was glad that I'd been able to witness this intense job before I stepped out of the profession for good.

The excitement soon made way for long hours of intense desk work. We were going to try and remand him in prison until the trial; there was a LOT to do. The PACE clock was ticking, and the whole department leapt into action, working ferociously to get all the material ready within 24 hours.

Two officers set out to custody for interview. Having spent a whole night with Rahul on bed watch, I was glad I didn't have to endure his theatrics.

"Let's hope it's going to be a no comment," someone said. I was certain it wouldn't be. In the end, I think the interview ran for close to three hours. It must have been incredibly frustrating.

I was in the office working on the various casefile forms. We had another little flurry of excitement when the dashcam footage from the traffic unit and some CCTV arrived. Everyone gathered around to watch the arrest. One of the CCTV cameras perfectly picked up the moment the suspect was rammed by a traffic vehicle just in front of the hospital. We watched as Rahul got out of the car and sprinted across the hospital grounds with officers in hot pursuit, his fisher's hat flying off his head. The officers quickly caught up with Rahul, tackled him to the ground, and arrested him.

"He runs exactly like Captain Jack Sparrow!" someone observed. They were absolutely right, and it took me a little while to get my giggles under control. I also noticed that he'd gained a few pounds since the last time I'd seen him, which made the whole scene even more laughable; a slightly overweight man running away from the police like a drunken pirate.

This was definitely one of the longer shifts I did. All told, I started at 8am and finished around 9pm. But the atmosphere was good in the office, and we all got takeaways delivered to the office while we kept working on the case-files. I left the office feeling tired but satisfied that this guy was going to be off the street for a while.

You might think that such a positive experience might have convinced me to change my mind about leaving the police. But, great though it was, it was just one case out of many – and there were plenty of other ones that reinforced to me that my decision was the right one. One of the last cases I was OIC for is a great example.

I can't really go into the specifics of the case, but the moment that's worth sharing here was my interview with the potential suspect – a man in his nineties with dementia.

The man was being invited in for a voluntary interview, rather than being arrested, but due to his being in hospital for several months, a lot of time had passed by the time we actually got to interview him. I felt strongly against proceeding with the criminal case, and was convinced that interviewing him was an absolute waste of time. We had no evidence for the crime we were investigating, and even if the man admitted to the offence in interview it would likely be inadmissible due to his dementia. Even if it was admissible, remember that a confession alone is not enough to convict someone. To me this was something adult social care should deal with now. But the inspector and sergeant remained adamant that due to the seriousness of the offence, an interview was warranted – more of the ass-covering police agenda.

The day of the interview finally came around, and I was dreading it. The duty solicitor who was present read through the pre-interview briefing.

"Are you joking? Excuse my language but...this is bullshit, right?" he said, eventually.

"I have to at least try and interview him," I answered as diplomatically as I could. I wholeheartedly agreed with the solicitor, but I had a job to do – and even though I was nearly finished in the police, I was determined to keep my integrity. So, in shuffled the old man.

At the start of each interview there is a part of a few minutes where you explain the process, caution someone and inform them of their rights. Even that part was pretty disastrous. The poor man simply couldn't understand the caution I was giving him. I remember that, every time I asked him whether he understood that he could not reply to a question if he didn't want to answer it, he would just reply "well, it depends on the question!"

Eventually, I decided we had got as far as possible with the explanation, and I started the main part of the interview. I asked him about the circumstances of the alleged offence.

He became very agitated and started shouting and slapping his hands on the table. Given his age and condition, I didn't feel particularly threatened; all I could think about was how ridiculous this whole situation was. After around ten minutes, I decided to call the interview off. I am certain that anyone who watched the interview would agree this person was not fit to be interviewed or stand trial. Thankfully, the sergeant was happy to drop the case after that. I was relieved the case was finally closed, but it was also confirmation for me that I had to leave this job. That interview was madness.

CHAPTER 40

LAST DAY

My last day as a detective at Thames Valley Police was anticlimactic. My colleagues were nice enough to have gotten me a card and some gifts – the usual stuff. Someone suggested going for a drink at the pub after work, and I had no objections. However, as the end of the shift rolled around everyone was busy with live jobs. I thought about staying, but my sergeant was insistent that I shouldn't force myself to stay late on my last day. So, I shook hands with my sergeant, said goodbye to my colleagues, and walked out the door.

Honestly, I preferred it that way. I appreciated the nice gestures from my colleagues, but leaving drinks can feel forced – especially when you have as little in common as I did with them. I drove home, and in many ways I didn't feel any different. It felt like I was going on holiday, not like I'd just left the job I'd dreamed of for years but which had turned out to be nothing like I'd imagined, and more than I could bear.

I wasn't granted much opportunity for reverie, though. As luck would have it, my dad had fallen ill and I was the only family member with free time on my hands, so I stayed with him for a week and helped him recover. After that, though, I started to think about the future.

I ended up taking three months off before I started looking for a new job. I needed the time to rest and recover. While in the police, my entire existence had either been work, sports, easy-watching television, or sleep. So I used the time to rediscover who I was outside of that. I cooked and read books. I walked around town and socialised. I saw my family and started to think about new hobbies and projects. If you ever get the chance to take a few months off from your job, I recommend it – without the crushing burnout and mental strain, if possible. It was wonderful.

I rather pointedly did not think about my time in the police at all for quite a while. I sort of pretended it hadn't happened, or had happened to someone else, and instead focused solely on myself and what I was going to do next. In many ways, it was freeing to no longer have a dream job. I think the title of 'dream job' had put a lot of pressure on my time at TVP – pressure to do well, pressure to enjoy it, and pressure to stay well after I should have thrown in the towel. I knew not to repeat those mistakes with my next job. Though a few reminders did crop up from time to time, such as my Diploma in Professional Policing Practice which showed up on my doormat one day. It turns out that even though I passed probation while working my notice, I still passed the DC DHEP course – and I'm proud of that. I did all the work, after all.

All of this leads me nicely to about three months after I'd left the police, when the boredom finally set in. I'd done enough sports, cooking, and reading. I wanted to get back to work. But what to do?

Part of the challenge with leaving the police is that it's one of those vocational jobs, like being a nurse, or a teacher, or a doctor. It becomes an enormous part of your identity, and it therefore becomes very difficult to imagine your life without it. Though that was a factor for me, I had only been there about two years – I still remembered life before being a detective, and I knew I could find a life afterwards, too.

I thought about what I'd enjoyed most about the police. Pretty soon, I realised it was the victim support element that I liked the most. Being there for someone at a low point in their life and doing your best to help them – that was the bit that made me come alive. Helping that woman pack to go to the refuge had been one of the times I was most in my element at TVP for precisely this reason. So I started looking for jobs where I could do that.

I looked for a while at private sector organisations with a link to policing. Lots of officers, when they reach retirement age, aren't quite ready to plant a garden and put their feet up – for a couple of reasons. Firstly, officers can retire earlier than other professions can, so retired officers are relatively young compared to other pensioners. And secondly, they're not generally the kind of people who enjoy sitting around doing what other people would call 'enjoying your retirement'. So many of them start companies that support the police. There was one called "Police Pass" that created training videos that we watched during our basic training at Sully, and I remember it because they were hilarious. They often featured ridiculous stories, delivered absolutely deadpan by these gentlemen in suits, that were plainly designed to make you smile. Examples included fictional scenarios about genitalia smashing into bus windows, Beyonce references, and stories about doing the 5am walk of shame home.

I also looked at charities, NGOs, and all sorts. I won't say where I ended up for anonymity's sake, but when I did start working again I went back to work part-time at first; I wasn't quite ready to go back full-time. However, I was back at work, feeling positive and recovered. And, inevitably, I found myself reflecting on my experience in TVP.

I don't miss it for a second, but neither do I regret joining, despite how it turned out. In the first place, it was an incredible experience to have lived. I've seen things and done things that I'll never do in another job again. Secondly, I grew a lot in that job. I know myself and my own limits much better now, physically and mentally, and have vowed never to push myself beyond them again. I'm much more aware of my mental health than I'd ever been before my time in TVP. I'd also discovered my likes and dislikes in a job, which made me more able to choose my next role. I now know that rigid and bureaucratic structures aren't for me. Following process for process' sake wasn't something I could do. I'm much more passionate about the spirit of the law than the letter of the law. I also want to be able to effect change if something isn't working, which you couldn't do in the police; you just had to accept that the system was broken and keep working with it anyway. I enjoy having freedom to take the initiative and to solve problems creatively.

I also found myself wanting to write down my experiences. I wanted that written record for myself, partly to process the experience and partly as a way not to forget the whirlwind of ups and downs I'd experienced. But I also wanted to share my experiences with other people.

I've noticed that the police are often glamourised. Their own recruitment materials certainly paint a much rosier picture than I experienced, for starters, and police documentaries show only the most interesting parts of the job, cutting out 99% of what police work is. Even 'gritty' shows like Happy Valley and Line of Duty paint a fictionalised version of the police that glosses over much of the experience– the bits that ultimately led to my resignation. It's why they're so fun and exciting to watch, but the rest of the story needs to be told.

I don't want other people to go through the same experience I did. I wonder how many other officers have done. How many joined up full of excitement, giving that ritualistic 'living the dream' response to their colleagues without a trace of irony, only to grow cynical and fed up with the reality of it. Certainly there were enough of them in TVP when I was there. But, as I mentioned before, they never left because it was a stable job with a good pension. To my former police colleagues, I want to say: if you're not enjoying your job, if it's crushing your soul, if it's making you feel miserable, you CAN get out and find another job. I did.

Printed in Dunstable, United Kingdom

71473566R00130